AMERICAN AUTHORS
AND CRITICS SERIES

GENERAL EDITOR
JOHN MAHONEY
University of Detroit

JOHN STEINBECK, 1961

JOHN STEINBECK

An Introduction and Interpretation

JOSEPH FONTENROSE

University of California

HOLT, RINEHART AND WINSTON, INC.

New York · Chicago · San Francisco · Toronto · London

Library of Congress Catalog Card Number: 63–16263
22878–0116

Barnes & Noble, Inc., is the exclusive distributor of the hard-bound edition of this title.

Acknowledgment is made to The Viking Press, Inc., and to William Heinemann, Ltd., for permission to quote from the following works by John Steinbeck: *Cup of Gold,* copyright 1929 by Robert M. McBride and Co., 1936 by John Steinbeck; *Sea of Cortez,* copyright 1941 by John Steinbeck and Edward F. Ricketts; and the following works copyrighted by John Steinbeck: *The Pastures of Heaven,* 1932, 1960; *To a God Unknown,* 1933, 1961; *Tortilla Flat,* 1935; *In Dubious Battle,* 1936; *Of Mice and Men,* 1937; *The Long Valley,* 1938; *The Grapes of Wrath,* 1939; *The Moon Is Down,* 1942; *Cannery Row,* 1945; *The Pearl,* 1945; *The Wayward Bus,* 1947; *Burning Bright,* 1950; *East of Eden,* 1952; *Sweet Thursday,* 1954; *The Short Reign of Pippin IV,* 1957; *The Winter of Our Discontent,* 1961. Also to The Viking Press, Inc., for permission to quote from John Steinbeck's letters quoted by Lewis Gannett in his Introduction to the Viking *The Portable Steinbeck,* 1946; and for permission to use two photographs of John Steinbeck for illustrations in this book.

Acknowledgments are also due to Harvard University Press for permission to quote from Arthur Lovejoy's translation of a letter of G. W. Leibniz published in Lovejoy's *The Great Chain of Being,* 1936. To McIntosh and Otis, Inc., for permission to quote from letters of John Steinbeck. To Random House, Inc., for quotations from *The Women at Point Sur,* by Robinson Jeffers. Copyright 1927 and renewed 1955 by Robinson Jeffers. Reprinted by permission of Random House, Inc.

ABOUT THE AUTHOR

JOSEPH FONTENROSE teaches at the University of California. He received the American Council of Learned Societies Fellowship for study in Greece, was Senior Classical Fellow at the American Academy in Rome, and studied again in Greece on a Guggenheim Fellowship. In addition to numerous articles and reviews in scholarly journals in the United States and abroad, his published works include *Python: A Study of Delphic Myth and Its Origins, The Cult and Myth of Pyrros at Delphi,* and *The Ritual Theory of Myth.*

PREFACE

IT IS HARDLY too much to say that John Steinbeck is now the most eminent of living American novelists. On July 6, 1962, as I was putting the finishing touches on the manuscript of this book, came the news of the death of William Faulkner, and just a year earlier Ernest Hemingway died. For a quarter century Faulkner, Hemingway, and Steinbeck were the three names that usually came to mind when one was asked who were the greatest living American novelists—though any such evaluative judgment might have been hotly disputed by partisans of other American novelists.

Then on October 23, 1962, John Steinbeck was chosen to receive the Nobel Prize for literature. That award established beyond doubt that Steinbeck holds a position in American letters which entitles his books to serious consideration. But even if he had never received the prize, the fact that several of his novels—among them *The Grapes of Wrath, In Dubious Battle,* and *Tortilla Flat*—have won a permanent place on the shelf of America's best books and are read and enjoyed all over the world would make him important. A writer of such stature and renown attracts critical attention, and recently the volume of Steinbeck criticism and scholarship has been increasing. If it is one criterion of greatness in a writer that no critic can comprehend the whole of his work or ever say the last word about it, then Steinbeck is surely a great writer and there will be no end to Steinbeck criticism, since every critical writer will judge his work from a different viewpoint.

That the writer of this Introduction and Interpretation is a classical scholar needs, I am sure, no apology. For the literary scholar, whatever his center of interest, has all literature for his province. In truth, I am not really so far out of my specialty as at first glance I may seem to be. My special field is mythology, which is not only a popular subject in present-day literary criticism, but has a particular relevance to Steinbeck studies. As the following pages will show, traditional myths and legends have much to do with the form and content of Steinbeck's fiction. True enough, Biblical and Arthurian themes predominate in his work, but Greek mythology is by no means absent. Political theory also has been one of my principal interests, and for that reason I have been greatly concerned with Steinbeck's theory of group organism, prominent in his earlier novels.

It has been a great pleasure to reread Steinbeck's works, and a pleasure and privilege to write this little book about them. It is principally a volume

Preface

of analysis, of appreciation, and of critical judgment, the latter not always laudatory (it grieves me to say), particularly with respect to Steinbeck's latest novels. I refrain, however, from pronouncing any book a "failure," believing it presumptuous of any critic to condemn a creative writer's work with such an Olympian judgment.

🙚 🙚

My sincere and cordial thanks are due to Frederic Carpenter, William Helmbold, Peter Lisca, and Ian Watt for reading and commenting on my first lucubrations in Steinbeck criticism (the present book has benefited much thereby); to John Steinbeck for comments on the aforesaid lucubrations, and for patient answering of questions; to his sister, Mrs. E. G. Ainsworth, for answering questions, for a photograph which appears as an illustration in this book, and for a big box of letters and clippings which provided material for my introductory chapter; to Elizabeth Otis of McIntosh and Otis for finding photographs and giving help; to Dorothy Hight Vera, feature editor of the Salinas *Californian*, for a recent photograph of the Steinbeck house; to Harvey Hall, Registrar of Stanford University, for information about Steinbeck's course of study at Stanford; to Professors Foster Provost of Duquesne University and John Mahoney of the University of Detroit, respectively former editor and present editor of the American Authors and Critics Series, for help, encouragement, and pleasant association; finally, to Elbert Epler and Joan Smyth of the editorial department of Barnes & Noble for careful editing and genial cooperation.

J. F.

CONTENTS

ILLUSTRATIONS

CHRONOLOGY

1902   John Ernst Steinbeck born February 27 in Salinas, California.

1919   Graduated from Salinas High School.

1920   Began intermittent attendance at Stanford University.

1924   First publications, "Fingers of Cloud" and "Adventures in Arcademy," in *The Stanford Spectator* (February, June).

1925   Left Stanford without a degree. Went to New York City and worked as construction laborer and reporter.

1926   Returned to California. Humorous verse published in *Stanford Lit* (March).

1929   *Cup of Gold* published.

1930   Married Carol Henning and began residence in Pacific Grove. First met Edward Ricketts.

1932   Moved to Los Angeles in summer. *The Pastures of Heaven* published.

1933   Returned to Pacific Grove early in year. *To a God Unknown* published. Two stories, the first two parts of *The Red Pony*, published in *North American Review* (November, December).

1934   Olive Hamilton Steinbeck, John's mother, died in February. "The Murder" selected as an O. Henry prize story.

1935   *Tortilla Flat* published, bringing immediate fame and financial success.

1936   *In Dubious Battle* published. Moved to Los Gatos. John Ernst Steinbeck, John's father, died in May. Articles, "The Harvest Gypsies," published in *San Francisco News* (October). Trip to Mexico.

1937   *Of Mice and Men* published in February. Went to New York and Pennsylvania to work on stage version, which was produced at Music Box Theatre in New York in November and won Drama Critics' Circle Award for that season. *The Red Pony*, in three parts, published. First trip to Europe. Late in year, went west from Oklahoma with migrants.

1938   *The Long Valley* and *"Their Blood Is Strong,"* pamphlet reprint of "The Harvest Gypsies," published.

1939   *The Grapes of Wrath* published.

1940   Won Pulitzer Prize for *The Grapes of Wrath*. With Ed Ricketts went to Gulf of California on "Western Flyer" to collect marine invertebrates, March–April.

1941   *Sea of Cortez* published.

1942   Separation and interlocutory divorce from Carol Henning. *The Moon Is Down* published. *Bombs Away* written for Army Air Corps.

1943   Married Gwyndolen Conger (Verdon) in March and began residence in New York. Spent several months in European war zone as correspondent for New York *Herald Tribune*.

1944   Son Thomas born. *Cannery Row* (dated 1945) published in December.

1945   *The Red Pony* republished with fourth chapter, "The Leader of the People." "The Pearl of the World" appeared in *Woman's Home Companion* magazine in December.

1946   Son John born.

1947   Trip to Russia with Robert Capa, August-September. *The Wayward Bus* and *The Pearl* published.

1948   Elected to American Academy of Letters. Divorced from Gwyndolen Conger. *A Russian Journal*, an account of his trip to Russia, published. Death of Ed Ricketts.

1950   *Burning Bright* published. Married Elaine Scott in December.

1951   *The Log from the Sea of Cortez* published, containing introduction and narrative from *Sea of Cortez* and biographical sketch "About Ed Ricketts."

1952   *East of Eden* published.

1954   *Sweet Thursday* published.

1957   *The Short Reign of Pippin IV* published.

1958   *Once There Was a War*, a collection of wartime dispatches, published.

1961   *The Winter of Our Discontent* published.

1962   *Travels with Charley* published. Received Nobel Prize for literature in December.

To Marie

And if I have done well, and as is fitting the story, it is that which I desired: but if slenderly and meanly, it is that which I could attain unto.

II MACCABEES 15:38

⤳ BIOGRAPHICAL INTRODUCTION

Soon after entering the Union in 1850 California began to assume an important place in American letters. Within two decades Joaquin Miller, Bret Harte, Mark Twain, and Ambrose Bierce had come to the state; and Robert Louis Stevenson reached Monterey in 1879. Before 1914 George Sterling, Frank Norris, Upton Sinclair, and Robinson Jeffers had become permanent residents of California, as had Miller before them. By 1900 a native writer of distinction, Jack London, had appeared. And on February 27, 1902, the year of Norris' early death, when Jack London was approaching his best period, John Steinbeck was born in Salinas, county seat of Monterey County.

His father's family, originally called Grossteinbeck, had come from Elberfeld (Wuppertal), about twenty miles east of the German city of Düsseldorf. Over half a century before John's birth, his grandfather, John Adolph, with an older brother accompanied their sister and her husband, a Lutheran missionary, to Jerusalem. There the Grossteinbeck brothers met and married the Dixon sisters, two young women from Massachusetts. After a few years, John Adolph came with his wife to the United States and settled first in New Jersey, and then in Florida, where John's father, John Ernst Steinbeck, was born at St. Augustine. The Civil War caught John Adolph in Florida, and he was drafted into the Confederate Army. Upon being discharged, he went with his family to Massachusetts and lived there for several years. In 1874 he crossed the country to California and established a flour mill in Hollister. His family followed, leaving Leominster, Massachusetts, on November 11, 1874, and joining him in Hollister the day before Thanksgiving. In 1890 John Ernst, then living in Monterey County, married Olive Hamilton, a schoolteacher.

Olive's father, Samuel Hamilton, an Ulsterman from Mulkeraugh, about eighteen miles northeast of Londonderry, came around the Horn to California as early as 1851; and he was soon afterwards joined by his wife Elizabeth (Liza), who crossed the Isthmus of Panama. Their early movements and places of residence in California are obscure. They were living in San Jose, where Olive was born, at the end of the Civil War. Later Samuel bought a ranch east of King City in Monterey County, where he and Liza reared a family of nine children, about whom we learn a good deal in his grandson's *East of Eden*. Olive, a schoolteacher at the age of seventeen, taught in one-room schoolhouses at Peachtree, Pleyto, and Big Sur before she married John Ernst Steinbeck and became mother of three daughters— Esther, Elizabeth, Mary—and one son, John Ernst, their third child. The Steinbecks lived for a time in King City and Paso Robles before settling down finally in Salinas. The elder John Ernst was in the flour-milling business, as John Adolph had been; later he became County Treasurer of Monterey County for eleven years, retiring from office a little over one year before his death in 1936, which occurred two years and three months after Olive Steinbeck's death.

❧ ☙

The younger John Ernst Steinbeck spent his boyhood in Salinas. With his family he made occasional exciting trips to San Francisco and more frequent trips to the Monterey peninsula—Monterey, Pacific Grove, Carmel—and to the Hamilton ranch near King City. He became familiar with Monterey County and the long Salinas Valley. From home or ranch he looked eastward to the Gabilan Mountains, warm and friendly, "full of sun and loveliness and a kind of invitation," as he says on the first page of *East of Eden;* and westward to the rugged, towering Santa Lucia Mountains, "dark and brooding—unfriendly and dangerous," suggesting death and making him shiver: they are the Great Mountains of *The Red Pony*. His native landscape moved him deeply, and from it he drew a special quality of mind, which has suffused his writings. It is like the quality visible in other California writers—Norris, London, Sterling, Jeffers —an awareness of and sympathy with the non-human, with the physical and biological environment in all its power and magnitude, dwarfing and absorbing humanity. The boy Steinbeck was sensitive to every feature of his native region; in *East of Eden* he says, "I remember my childhood names for grasses and secret flowers. I remember where a toad may live and what time the birds awaken in the summer—and what trees and seasons smelled like. . . ."

He went through the Salinas schools and in 1919 graduated from Salinas High School. He was always a good student, eager to learn both in and out of school, interested in books, music, science, religion, and sports. Intellectual interests were never discouraged in the Steinbeck family: not only had Olive Steinbeck been a teacher, but her father was a well-read man, as we learn in *East of Eden*. So John heard good music and read good books, discovering Malory, Andersen, Stevenson, Lewis Carroll's Alice books. He attended Episcopal Sunday School, since this Steinbeck family had adopted the Hamiltons' church; there and at home he acquired a taste for scripture which had a profound effect upon his literary style and form.

Between 1920 and 1925 he attended Stanford University intermittently, never fulfilling the requirements for graduation. There he took a year course (three terms) in classical literature, in which he was especially impressed by the Greek historians and Plato's dialogues, and an introductory course in zoology, a subject to which he devoted much time and study in later years. His classes in English literature may have first introduced him to certain authors, but at present nobody, not even Steinbeck, can say for certain when he first encountered one writer or another, whether in his assigned reading or outside of class or before he matriculated at Stanford. By 1925 he had read widely in English, American, and European literature; he enjoyed Milton, Browning, Thackeray, George Eliot, Hardy, D. H. Lawrence, Jeffers, Flaubert, Dostoevsky, among others, including a few writers for whom his enthusiasm later waned—James Branch Cabell, Norman Douglas, and Sherwood Anderson.

In the intervals between terms of attendance at Stanford he worked at various jobs on ranches and road gangs, in sugar mills and the like, acquiring knowledge of the lower strata of society. He could get on well with all sorts of persons, and he discovered the genuine human qualities of humble people while working with them; he had no snobbery in him.

Steinbeck also took classes in writing at Stanford, and began at that time to send manuscripts to magazines, according to H. T. Moore, but he received only rejection slips in return. A story "Fingers of Cloud," which showed promise, was published in *The Stanford Spectator,* and so was a short satirical sketch. A few verse parodies appeared in *Stanford Lit.* This, of course, was non-remunerative writing. In the fall of 1925 Steinbeck went to New York City, hoping to make his living there as a writer. He arrived with just three dollars in his pocket, and his brother-in-law, E. G. Ainsworth, found him a job pushing wheelbarrows of concrete for the construction of Madison Square Garden. Then he worked as a reporter for the New York *American,* a position which his uncle Joe Hamilton, an advertising man, found for him. He was not a very good reporter, he tells us, and was soon discharged. After trying free-lance writing in New York for a short time, he returned, discouraged, to California. For three years, periods of temporary employment alternated with periods entirely devoted to writing; and he moved from place to place, to San Francisco, Monterey, Salinas, Lake Tahoe, writing novels and stories that no publisher would buy. Finally, in 1929, McBride accepted and published *Cup of Gold,* a fictional biography of Henry Morgan the pirate, which Steinbeck wrote during two winters spent at Lake Tahoe, first as caretaker of a lodge (he was discharged when a tree fell on the building) and then as worker in a fish hatchery. *Cup of Gold,* however, brought him little money, and the next six years were no easier; for although *The Pastures of Heaven* and *To a God Unknown* were published in 1932 and 1933, not many copies of either were sold. In 1933 and 1934 he sold five stories to *North American Review,* including two parts of *The Red Pony.* In those depression times only the great popular monthlies and weeklies paid much for stories, and the *Review* was not one of them; still, "The Murder" was selected as an O. Henry prize story for 1934.

In 1930, Steinbeck married Carol Henning. His father gave the young couple a house in Pacific Grove and a monthly allowance of $25, and often this allowance was all they had to live on. The frequent discouragements of the next few years are reflected in the story of Tom Talbot, a struggling writer, and his wife, Mary, in a chapter of *Cannery Row.* Except for a brief interval in Los Angeles, the Steinbecks lived in Pacific Grove until 1936. Another important event in Steinbeck's life also occurred in 1930: in a dentist's waiting room he met Edward Ricketts, owner and operator of a small commercial biological laboratory on the waterfront of Monterey. In "About Ed

Ricketts," written two years after Ricketts' death in 1948, Steinbeck tells the story of the close and personally significant friendship then begun. He went often to the laboratory, talked with Ricketts on all sorts of subjects, listened to his records, drank with him (both being devoted to beer, wine, whisky, and the like), and enjoyed many uproarious parties celebrated at the lab. The association with Ricketts stimulated Steinbeck's interest in biology; out of it came that biological view of man which pervades the novels of Steinbeck's best period, and Ricketts was the model for important characters in three novels (*In Dubious Battle, Cannery Row, Sweet Thursday*) and a short story ("The Snake").

In 1935 *Tortilla Flat* was published, pleased the reading public, and immediately established Steinbeck as an important American writer. Then hard times vanished for good. From that year Steinbeck became increasingly affluent as each successive novel became a bestseller. His novels won prizes, became book-club choices, were made into movies, were reprinted as paperbacks. The story of Steinbeck as a novelist is told in the following chapters, and there remains little to tell here.

After the success of *Tortilla Flat*, Steinbeck and his wife moved to a ranchhouse near Los Gatos in the Santa Cruz mountains. Later in the year (1936) they went to Mexico, the first of many trips that Steinbeck has taken to foreign lands—France, Italy, Greece, Russia, Scandinavia, England, and the Hamiltons' ancestral home in Northern Ireland. He is an inveterate traveler, so much so that after 1939 he was seldom home. His wife divorced him in 1942, and in March, 1943, he married Gwyndolen Conger (Verdon), who became the mother of his only children, Tom and John. This second marriage marks a dividing line in Steinbeck's career. With it he ceased to be a Californian. Soon after the wedding he went to the European war theater as a correspondent for the New York *Herald Tribune*. Upon his return to the United States late in the year, he established his residence in New York (and now has homes in Manhattan and on Long Island), although he has continued to travel and has made lengthy visits to Paris. In 1948, his second marriage ended in divorce. He married Elaine Scott in December, 1950, and in *Travels with Charley*, written ten years later, he lets us know that in this marriage he has been happy.

The shift of residence from California to New York has manifestly affected the quality of Steinbeck's fiction. The novels published since 1943 (with the exception of the first, *Cannery Row*, which, though showing signs of change, still reflects the earlier period) have been distinctly different from those published before 1943; and no doubt it was mainly the earlier novels which won Steinbeck election to the American Academy of Letters in 1948 and the Nobel Prize in 1962.

❧ ☙

Peter Lisca has accurately pointed out that Steinbeck's works show his persistent interest in both the biological and the mythopoeic heritage of man. Each, biology and myth, is a poetic, creative factor in Steinbeck's fiction: intermeshed, they provide the substructure of his great novels of the thirties and will be my principal concern in the following pages. We shall see how the conceptions of ecological community and of group organism, which Steinbeck derived from his study of biology, assume greater and greater importance in his novels from *Cup of Gold,* where they are barely perceptible, to *The Grapes of Wrath,* where they reach a climax; and how they then recede gradually until in *East of Eden* they are nearly lost to view— although they are still visible in Steinbeck's last novel. Myth has been a more constant factor, profoundly affecting the form and content of all his novels since 1929. In most of them we may see myth as a palimpsest upon which Steinbeck has inscribed a realistic tale of contemporary men. It is as though a writer, using a palimpsest, should retain words, sentences, even paragraphs of the original text, merely retouching them before incorporating them into the new text superimposed. As Charles Moorman has expressed it in his study of three contemporary poets, *Arthurian Triptych,* "the myth brings stature, order, and meaning to the modern writer's attempts to order the chaotic world of his own time."

ᵉ§ **THE FIRST NOVELS**

CUP OF GOLD

STEINBECK's first novel, *Cup of Gold*, published in August, 1929, has the subtitle "A Life of Sir Henry Morgan, *Buccaneer*, with Occasional Reference to History," and thus we are warned not to read it as an authentic biography of Morgan. The story begins in Wales when Dafydd, returning after years spent in the Indies, inspired fifteen-year-old Henry Morgan with a desire to go to the Caribbean. Soon Henry left home for Cardiff and took passage as a hand on the "Bristol Girl." When the ship reached Barbados, he found himself an indentured slave, a victim of the system by which the plantations got workers. Henry was fortunate in his master, James Flower, a wealthy eccentric with intellectual pretensions. Serving as Flower's companion, Henry gradually acquired power over him and the plantation, accumulating wealth by devious means. Flower freed him before his term of indenture was finished, and at once Henry set out to acquire a ship and join the buccaneers. He soon won success and reputation, becoming commander of the whole Brotherhood of Buccaneers. Hearing of a beautiful woman in Panama called La Santa Roja, he became obsessed with the desire of possessing her, led his buccaneers across the isthmus, and took the city. But when he saw the woman, whose name was Ysobel, she failed to meet the requirements of his dream, and his attempts to possess her were half-hearted and unsuccessful. After plundering Panama and returning across the isthmus, Morgan sailed away with

7

all the loot while his buccaneers lay in drunken slumber on shore. He went to Jamaica and then to England, where Charles II knighted him and made him lieutenant-governor of Jamaica with authority to suppress piracy. Henry married his cousin, Elizabeth, daughter of Sir Edward Morgan, former lieutenant-governor of Jamaica. The story ends with Henry on his deathbed as the deeds and thoughts of his life cluster about him.

At a rough estimate, the story contains about nine parts fiction to one of history. Henry Morgan may have been indentured; he did become leader of the buccaneers, took Panama, and was appointed lieutenant-governor of Jamaica. The principal episodes have some foundation in fact. Exquemelin, one of Morgan's men, tells about a beautiful and virtuous Spanish woman whom Morgan treated with great respect and wanted to marry, although he already had a wife and she a husband. After steadfastly rejecting his proposals she was finally ransomed, her virtue intact. This woman Steinbeck has transformed into La Santa Roja, robbing her of her virtue in the process by mingling her with "A Lady in Infra-Red," subject of an unpublished story which he wrote when a student at Stanford.

On the historical foundation Steinbeck built a superstructure of fiction, which superficially appears to be a romance of the Spanish Main, a genre popular in the twenties. Rafael Sabatini's *Captain Blood* appeared in 1922, and the popular movie version of it about 1925. Steinbeck's Henry Morgan owes several traits to Peter Blood, who also seems to be derived in part from the historical Morgan. Both Blood and Steinbeck's Morgan, forced into indentures, become valuable to their superiors (Blood as physician to the governor), gain fame as pirate chiefs, and finally become governors of Jamaica. Each named a ship after his ladylove, Blood's "Arabella," Morgan's "Elizabeth" (and Blood had an "Elizabeth" under his command). In fact, simply considered as an adventure story of buccaneering on the Spanish Main, *Cup of Gold* is fully as entertaining as *Captain Blood*. It may even stand comparison with Kingsley's *Westward Ho!*, which has also left its mark on *Cup of Gold*. As John Oxenham and Salvation Yeo inspired Amyas Leigh with a desire to cross the sea and fight Spaniards in the Caribbean, so Dafydd inspired Henry Morgan. As Oxenham made a daring expedition to find a beautiful Spanish woman and crossed the isthmus with gold bars and silver plate, so did Henry Morgan (I refer to the fictional rather than to the historical events) —but, of course, the outcome was different: Oxenham was not Steinbeck's Morgan, and Señora Xararte was another woman than La

8

Santa Roja. Stevenson's *Treasure Island,* loved by the boy Steinbeck, left its mark, too, on *Cup of Gold:* there are traces of Jim Hawkins in Steinbeck's Morgan and of Billy Bones in Dafydd.

Nevertheless, *Cup of Gold* is a buccaneering romance with a difference. It stands in about the same relation to *Captain Blood* as do James Branch Cabell's novels to *The Prisoner of Zenda.* The youthful Cabell wanted to write romances like Anthony Hope's; Steinbeck, however, did not want to write novels like Sabatini's but like Cabell's, and *Cup of Gold* shows Cabell's influence. Many a sentence has a Cabellesque ring. Morgan's "I must be sailing outward to the Indies" and "I *must* be off a-buccaneering," and his "desire for a thing he could not name," recall Cabell's heroes, who eternally have nameless desires and must follow after them. When Morgan tries to shake off his obsession by taking Maracaibo, his action is punctuated by parenthetical refrains: "There is a woman in the Cup of Gold, and she is lovely as the sun," with Cabell-like variations thereon. Like Cabell's Jurgen, Morgan saw Helen, in the person of La Santa Roja, and spoke with Merlin; his Merlin is a seventeenth-century worthy, a seer and bard, obviously the Arthurian wizard reborn. Above all, the central theme is Cabellian: the sordid reality of man's achievement is opposed to his youthful dream. The hero desires adventure, power, wealth, a paragon of beautiful womanhood; he gets them, but the achievement proves unsatisfactory and empty. Though the world envies his success, "he only can realize his true failure," as Merlin told Morgan. This naive cynicism is what makes the difference between Cabell and his romantic predecessors, between Steinbeck's *Cup of Gold* and its buccaneering forerunners, where only exciting adventures mattered. But *Cup of Gold* is not an imitation of *Jurgen,* and Cabell's is not the only influence upon it.

As a Faustian hero Morgan looks more like Peer Gynt than like Jurgen. He has a purpose and drive that Peer Gynt lacks; yet the parallels are numerous enough to indicate that Steinbeck had Peer Gynt in mind. Like Ibsen's hero, Morgan has youthful dreams of grandeur; is boastful, conceited, and erratic; wins riches overseas by evil means; and finally becomes isolated from his fellows. In dark Paulette we may see both the Troll King's daughter and Moorish Anitra; and as Anitra repelled Peer Gynt with a whip, La Santa Roja repelled Morgan with a long pin. Morgan's four times repeated and increasingly exaggerated tale of his imaginary affair with his childhood sweetheart, Elizabeth, who becomes a princess the fourth time, recalls Peer Gynt's tale about his affair with a girl of royal blood; and both Morgan and Peer made their boasts while drinking. Near the end of his life Peer Gynt was reproached by the thoughts and deeds that he did not think and do; Morgan was reproached on his deathbed by the thoughts and deeds that he did think and do. Solveig (Ibsen's Margaret) saved Peer from the Button Molder; the vision of Elizabeth banished the faceless creatures that haunted Morgan.

However, the title *Cup of Gold,* the central cup symbol accompanied by frequent round and concave images, and the climactic event, the taking of Panama, the "Cup of Gold," indicate that the Grail legend provided the central structure of this novel. In the heap of loot taken at Panama, Morgan found a golden cup: "It was a lovely, slender chalice with long curved handles and a rim of silver." The Cup of Gold was "a cloud city, an eerie, half-unearthly place, and armed with lightnings," Grail and Gralsburg in one. And La Santa Roja was the Repanse de Joie of this Grail paradise: "she was Mary come to live on earth again." So Morgan is a knight who has gone in search of the Grail; his buccaneers are companion knights of the Round Table.

Yet it is Faust, not Galahad or Percival, who goes in quest of the Grail. The Grail represents romance, youthful dreams of adventure, conquest, fortune. The Faust theme (which Lisca has perceived) gives a cynical twist to the Grail theme, revealing the frailties and follies of the hero, and depreciating the objects of his desire. When all is done, the victor finds that he did not win what he wanted. Morgan's father said of him, ". . . he runs about sticking his finger into pot after pot of cold porridge, grandly confident that each one will prove the pottage of his dreaming . . ." Merlin said that "boys who wanted the moon . . . sometimes caught a firefly." The golden chalice which Morgan found in the Panama loot was a bauble: "Around its outer edge four grotesque lambs chased each other, and inside, on the bottom, a naked girl lifted her arms in sensual ecstasy." The golden lambs suggest the Golden Fleece: Jason, winning it, has won nothing.

Panama, the Gralsburg, is Troy too. Sitting near "a Greek tripod of black iron," which held a copper brazier, Merlin reminded the boy Henry that he was descended from Trojans, whose wanderings "when Pergamus fell in" brought them to Britain. Thus through Geoffrey of Monmouth's Brutus the Trojan legend is linked to Arthur and the Grail. A second link is seen in the name of Morgan's first pirate ship, the "Ganymede," named for the Trojan who became cupbearer of the gods. Morgan supposed that Ysobel, the Red Saint, "is as jealously guarded as was Helen," and Cœur de Gris, Morgan's companion, thought that "sometime, the Cup of Gold may go the way of Troy town on account of her." Panama-Troy fell in flames, and like the Achaeans, the buccaneers committed unspeakable crimes as they sacked the town. Helen was taken—and Steinbeck's Faust was disappointed in the vision; this is an early instance of Steinbeck's myth inversion. Ysobel's name (the Spanish form of "Elizabeth") unites her to the four Elizabeths: Morgan's childhood sweetheart, wife, mother, and first ship (before he became a pirate). She is the Cabell woman, both Helen, the object of every man's desire, and Dame Lisa, the practical, scolding wife whom he marries.

The Grail and Troy themes are merged in *Cup of Gold* with the myth of the dying-and-rising god or year-spirit. In 1920 Jessie Weston's *From Ritual to Romance* traced the legend of Grail, Fisher King, and Waste Land to the myths of Adonis, Attis, and other dying fertility gods of the ancient Near East, thus bringing Arthurian legend under the shadow of Frazer's *Golden Bough*. Directly or indirectly her book influenced Steinbeck, as it did T. S. Eliot; and Steinbeck was acquainted with Frazer's book. We first meet Henry Morgan when "Night drew down like a black cowl, and Holy Winter sent his nuncio to Wales." Images of blackness and allusions to night, winter, and cold fill the first chapter; thereafter images of black and white alternate with and oppose each other. The dying-god theme becomes explicit in grandmother Gwenliana's prophecy. She spoke of Annwn, Chaos or Death, who often "set its fanged maw to entrap" Henry's life, but for a thousand ages Henry had eluded Annwn to live again and again, and would continue to do so for another thousand. Henry would triumph and "The government of islands and continents shall be thine, and thou shalt bring justice and peace to them." When Henry left home, his father predicted that he would return "when the Spring comes in," and told his wife that she must believe in Henry's coming. Fifteen years later, "Spring had come to Cambria, welling up out of the Indies. . . . Old Robert liked to think, and then came curiously to believe, that his son sent the Spring to Cambria out of the tropic places." Henry went to sea as winter came in, and the ship passed through terrible storms; the brown sea birds were the souls of drowned sailors. Wanting to be a god that rode the storm, Henry "cried for the shoulders of omnipotence . . ." "Then, as quickly as the devil servants of the year had rushed at . . . [the ship], they slunk away, leaving a clear, clean sea," and Morgan came "to the home of Summer, whence it goes yearly to the northern places." At this moment the bubble of myth is pricked: Morgan learned that he was an indentured slave of James Flower—such is the bloom in this land of summer.

Steinbeck's romance of buccaneering adventure, therefore, is expressed in terms of four intertwined myths, to which are subordinated several minor folkloristic themes: Argonauts, Odysseus, Orpheus, Pan, Glendower's magical power, Druid mysteries, sailors' lore, ghost lore, Tylwyth Teg, El Dorado. Set in counterpoint is a realistic narrative of actual buccaneering as historical records reveal it. We move pleasantly on paths of myth, and then suddenly we are looking at the indenture system, black slaves in cages, methods of breeding slaves, imperialism, Spanish cruelty, English rapacity, betrayal of comrades, miseries of war and pillage. Of course, bloodshed, torture, and pillage enter into romances, but an aura of glamor surrounds them; we do not see them as they really are. In *Cup of Gold* we see the realities of war and pillage. Finally, by imposing the Faust theme on myths of quest, combat, and resurrection, Steinbeck shows us that the hero's triumphs are illusory. The Grail is but a golden cup; the knight who wins it is more likely to be Sir Henry Morgan than Sir Galahad. The Trojan War, like any war, was Hell.

We thus perceive that romance is the perception of events through rose-colored glasses of myth and legend: myth makes the difference between history or purely realistic narrative on the one hand and romance on the other. But our perception of this is clouded by Cabell's theme of the vanity of human achievement. The debunking of romance and the romantic hero is confused with the debunking of aspirations. Merlin said that Henry would become a great man if only he remained a child, and he referred not to childhood's innocent wisdom but to its folly. A false opposition of great man to wise man gets in the way of the contrast between the hero of romance and the real warrior or pirate.

Cup of Gold is not a great novel, but it tells a good story and contains some passages of good writing. It was an auspicious start for an aspiring novelist, and Steinbeck learned much about his craft from writing it. It reveals a good deal of the later Steinbeck, for many a favorite theme and character type appear here for the first time. Although Steinbeck had not yet met Ed Ricketts, he already makes evident an interest in biology, as in many unusual similes (e.g., "the farmhouses huddled like feeding bugs") which reveal accurate observations of living creatures. Something like the group organism of later novels makes its appearance in the Brotherhood of Buccaneers, a band of men sharing a common purpose, so united and disciplined that Mansveldt planned to convert it into a republic. Here, too, are the Steinbeck themes of loneliness, mystic identity with the whole world (notice the great Tone at the end), woman's secret knowledge, the speed of rumor, degeneration caused by too much security. Visible here are Steinbeck's interests in social justice, Greek and Latin literature, occult powers, the inner life of children. And in this, his first novel, we meet the Virgin Whore, the prostitute, the competent mother, the religious bigot, the madman, the wealthy amateur scientist, and the wizard-seer—recurring character types in Steinbeck's novels.

TO A GOD UNKNOWN

As *Cup of Gold* grew out of a story called "A Lady in Infra-Red," *To a God Unknown* grew out of a story called "The Green Lady." For five years Steinbeck worked upon it at intervals, and it was published in 1933, a year after publication of *The Pastures of Heaven*. But I follow Peter Lisca's example of putting it second in order of discussion, since Steinbeck had written a whole draft called "To an Unknown God" before he began work on *The Pastures*.

The story begins in Vermont about 1903. Joseph Wayne, one of four brothers, received his father's blessing and left for California, where he acquired land in the Valley of Nuestra Señora (Jolon Valley). When he received the news of his father's death, he fancied that his father's spirit had crossed the country and entered a large oak tree near his house. Then he called his brothers (Thomas, Burton, Benjamin) to him, and they took land next to his, forming a family community. In a pine grove on a ridge, Joseph and Thomas discovered a glade which contained a huge rock of strange shape and a spring which flowed from a small cave in the side of the rock. Thereafter with increasing seriousness Joseph practiced a cult of oak and rock. He married Elizabeth McGreggor, the young schoolteacher, who bore him a son the next summer. Joseph set the baby in the oak tree as a ritual act, although his pious brother Burton protested. Burton, long offended by Joseph's paganism, now girdled the oak and moved to Pacific Grove. Hitherto the winter rains had been plentiful and the land flourished, but the winter which followed the oak's death was dry. Joseph lost Elizabeth when she was killed in a fall from the rock in the glade. The drought continued until the land became so dry that the Waynes had to leave their homes and drive their cattle to the San Joaquin River. Joseph stayed on the ranch, abandoning the house and living in the glade until at last the spring dried up. On New Year's Day he mounted the rock and cut his wrists. As he died he felt that he had become the rain, and the needed rain began to pour at that moment.

Although *To a God Unknown* lapses occasionally into bad writing and sentimentality, it greatly surpasses *Cup of Gold* in prose style, plot structure, characterization, invention, and imaginative sweep. Joseph Wayne is a strong character, convincingly drawn. Rama, Thomas's wife, said,

> "I do not know whether there are men born outside humanity, or whether some men are so human as to make others seem unreal. Perhaps a godling lives on earth now and then. Joseph has strength beyond vision of shattering, he has the calm of mountains, and his emotion is as wild and fierce and sharp as the lightning and just as reasonless as far as I can see or know."

Thomas, oldest of the brothers, "had a strong kinship with all kinds of animals," and a remarkable knack of making friends with raccoons, coyotes, and other beasts. Burton was a devout evangelical Protestant, a "strong man in the Lord," but a "weak man in the stomach," who shunned all carnal pleasures and hated all rituals, Catholic or pagan. Benjamin, the youngest, was a drunkard and seducer of girls, irresponsible, helpless, dishonest—and yet "everyone loved Benjy and excused and guarded him."

In *To a God Unknown*, Biblical legend assumes the position that Arthurian legend holds in *Cup of Gold*. The central core is the Joseph story from Genesis. Of several brothers the youngest are named Joseph and Benjamin. Joseph as favorite son received his father's blessing, putting his hand under the old man's thigh (see Genesis 47:29): "Come to me, Joseph. Put your hand here—no, here. My father did it this way. A custom so old cannot be wrong. Now, leave your hand there!" Benjamin was the protected youngest son. Joseph's father was a white-bearded patriarch, ruling his family in the tribal manner. A hint of quarreling between brothers occurs at the beginning of the story: "Have you an anger for your brothers, Joseph? Is there some quarrel I haven't heard about?" Joseph left his native land for a distant and richer country. He had his brothers settle beside him in a patriarchal community, which he ruled. He took a wife in the new land. His father remained in the old country and was buried with his ancestors. Several prosperous years were followed by a barren period.

To this point the story of Joseph Wayne runs parallel to the story of Joseph, Jacob's son. The latter-day Joseph, however, resisted the paisanos' prophecy of coming drought and did not provide in the fat years for the lean. At this point Joseph is transformed into Jesus, although he has had a Jesus character from the first. The father, John, was his son's forerunner, being of like character and intuitions; the rot was already in him, according to Burton. Joseph, who has the name of Mary's husband, married Elizabeth, and her son was named John: the Holy Family is merged with John the Baptist's. Joseph's brother is Thomas, apprehensive and uncertain. Joseph settled in the Valley of Our Lady; when he first came, he mated symbolically with the land: "He flung himself face downward on the grass and pressed his cheek against the wet stems. His fingers gripped the wet grass. . . . For a moment the land had been his wife." At the wedding of Joseph and Elizabeth, she made a silent prayer to Jesus, "and when she drew a picture of the Christ in her mind, He had the face, the youthful beard, the piercing puzzled eyes of Joseph. . . ." She thought, "I'm praying to my own husband." Sometime later when Joseph put a cold wet hand on Elizabeth's head, she was reminded of the bishop's cold hand at her confirmation, when she thought that the shivers running down her back were the infusion of the Holy Spirit. The priest, Father Angelo, was glad that Joseph had no message, "else there might be a new Christ here in the West." When drought has devastated the land, the story of the Passion begins. It is prefigured by the three crosses which a strange old man had placed near a cliff edge on the coast; there he had buried three drowned sailors: "Two were dark men, and one was light. The light one wore a saint's medallion on a string around his neck." Juanito, Joseph's paisano friend, looked at the sleeping Joseph in the glade, not long before the end, and saw in him the crucified Christ with the same look of disappointment and weariness in his face. Finally, Joseph, lying on the rock with his slashed wrist outstretched, died to save his land.

Joseph's sacrifice, however, is not the Christian sacrifice—or it is something more than that. Joseph is in part the Fisher King, as Lisca has pointed out; his scorched earth is the Waste Land. And the name Joseph may have a third reference, to Joseph of Arimathea, receiver of the Grail, ancestor or brother-in-law of the Fisher King. Yet in the Grail legend it was not the Fisher King's death but his recovery that brought life back to the land. Steinbeck had in mind not so much the Fisher King himself as his pagan antecedents, the myths and rituals of Jessie Weston's *From Ritual to Romance.* A reviewer said that *To a God Unknown* "might be considered a modern appendix to 'The Golden Bough.' " Joseph is a Frazerian divine king who must die because he has lost his divine potency.

Joseph is therefore the dying king whose death renews the land, rather than the dying god whose resurrection restores life (though the god may be derived from the king). The story follows the life history of a god-king, a ritual sequence rather than a myth—it matters little that there is no real evidence for "the king must die," since Steinbeck simply used the Frazerian construction for his own purpose.

> On the old farm in Vermont his father had merged with the land until he became the living symbol of the unit, land and its inhabitants. That authority passed to Joseph. He spoke with the sanction of the grass, the soil, the beasts wild and domesticated; he was the father of the farm.

Joseph had his mystic union with the earth. He passionately promoted fertility and cut off the barren. His marriage was part of his role: "Everything on the land is reproducing. I am the only sterile thing. I need a wife." So his marriage to Elizabeth (the name used five times in *Cup of Gold*) was a *hieros gamos,* a sacred marriage meant to fertilize the whole realm. The long symbolic passage (which has annoyed some readers) about Joseph's going through the pass with Elizabeth is fertility ritual and a *rite de passage,* complete with scapegoat sacrifice. For Benjamin was killed at this time while engaged in the sex act, representing the mock king who was killed to insure the safety of the real king; and the killer was not punished, but vanished for a time like the killers of the sacred ox in Athens. Rama said, "When we have buried him, we'll never mention Benjy any more. In a year we will forget he ever lived." The mock king reigned briefly in luxury, during a temporary absence or abdication of the real king (Joseph was absent in Monterey, getting married), had his choice of women, and was then killed and forgotten.

Plentiful rains followed the wedding, the crops were good, the cattle increased, and Joseph too was fruitful. The first November rains immediately followed the shooting of a hawk and killing of a pig, both of which Joseph hung on the oak tree, smearing the bark with pig's blood. Then came the New Year fiesta. The Indians and paisanos gathered on the ranch; Father Angelo celebrated Mass on a temporary altar under the oak; Joseph poured a libation of wine on the earth and on the tree, and offered meat to the tree; everyone feasted, drank wine, and danced, reaching a high pitch of excitement;

and on that day Elizabeth told Joseph of her pregnancy. The fiesta ended in a rainstorm, announced by thunder and lightning.

In the summer a son was born and Joseph himself was midwife. He set the baby in the tree crotch. After Burton girdled the oak, drought came. Late in the autumn Elizabeth died at the rock in the glade; a little rain fell, but not enough. That night Rama came to Joseph's bed: the king must remain potent to save the land ("This is a need," Rama said). But rainless days followed, and the land became increasingly dry through the next year. Joseph attributed the fault to himself; the king's power was failing: "I was appointed to care for the land, and I have failed." On New Year's Day, when the spring in the glade ran dry, he first sacrificed a calf without result, and then, lying on the rock which he called the heart of the land and source of its living seed, he sacrificed himself. And then the rain came.

Joseph's sacrifice was prefigured in the daily sacrifice made to the setting sun by a strange old man on the coast, who claimed to be "the last man in the western world to see the sun. After it is gone to everyone else, I see it for a little while." Every evening as the sun sank into the ocean he killed some animal, squirrel or rabbit or pig, on a slab of stone near his hut, which was perched on a cliff above the surf. And some day when all conditions were right, he intended to be the sacrifice. He thought that his sacrifices might help the sun, and "In the moment," he said, "I am the sun. . . . I burn in the death."

Joseph represents natural religion as opposed to the ascetic Christianity of his brother Burton. He brought together ancestor worship, tree and rock worship, fertility rituals, divine king, and dying god, exactly as the heathen have always done. As he saw it, cruel and inhuman powers are part of the whole. All gods are finally one god: the whole world is one living being. His paganism became pantheism: the World-God is the God Unknown. For epigraph Steinbeck used a shortened version of Rig-Veda 10:121, a hymn addressed "to Who?" and ending with the verse, "Who is the God to whom we shall offer sacrifice?" The poet calls him "God over Gods"; the world is his body; he can hurt us, since "His shadow is life, his shadow is death." The title also suggests the altar to the Unknown God which Paul found in Athens (Acts 17:23). The two sources of the title correspond to the pagan-Christian tension in the novel, as Lisca points out. Yet Paul and the Vedic poet expressed identical conceptions of deity: God made the world and everything in it; he is Lord of the world; he is the giver of life; he is everything. The pantheistic theme links pagan and Christian forms of belief to the religious ideas of India, in which

17

Steinbeck has shown interest. Joseph's Vedanta-like identity with the world is symbolized in his vision of his relaxed body as a world that endures for a million years and is then suddenly wiped out at the will of the brain overlooking it. And he said as he died, "I am the land . . . and I am the rain. The grass will grow out of me in a little while." We need not ask whether Joseph's rituals and sacrifices really affected the weather. These acts, performed at every juncture in the seasonal and weather cycles, expressed his harmony with nature, being themselves part of the process. For Steinbeck this seems to be true of all ritual acts.

The unity of the whole is reflected in the unity of parts. The idea of group organism has a larger place in this novel than in *Cup of Gold*. The Wayne patriarchal community is itself a single organism, and temporary groupings may become single organisms for the period of their duration. At the New Year fiesta guitars were tuning up, "bringing their rhythms together, feeling for a mood, so that when the dancing started they might be one passionate instrument." The dancing began; the crowd grew; soon everybody moved to the rhythm.

> One man had been notable for his height, another for the deepness of his voice; one woman had been beautiful, another ugly and fat, but that was changing. The dancers lost identity. Faces grew rapt, shoulders fell slightly forward, each person became a part of the dancing body, and the soul of the body was the rhythm.

If Henry Morgan resembles Ibsen's Peer Gynt, Joseph Wayne resembles Ibsen's Brand, and like Brand he died on the heights. But it is Robinson Jeffers' *The Women at Point Sur,* I believe, that affected *To a God Unknown* directly—and Jeffers' poem too was apparently influenced by *Brand*. A reviewer justly observed that *To a God Unknown* resembles a novelized version of a Jeffers poem. We are in the same Santa Lucia mountains, which the boy Steinbeck found hostile and menacing, and we once cross the range to the steep and rugged coast south of Point Sur, where Joseph met the strange old cultist, who in some respects resembles Jeffers' visionary Onorio Vasquez. Joseph Wayne strongly recalls Barclay, who abandoned his Christian ministry for a religion of nature and identified himself with God and the world:

> " 'I am God: but I am secret': and he said:
> 'You are atoms of humanity and all humanity
> A cell of my body: . . .' "

18

Barclay also taught that the World-God is indifferent to man's values: nothing is really evil, or good either. His religion was pantheistic and Dionysiac, with overtones of Vedanta and the Nirvana doctrine. He died in a waste place in the hills, "Smeared with the blood of sacrifice," which flowed from wounds self-inflicted on his hands. Joseph Wayne is certainly not a copy of Barclay, though he has taken several traits from him. In the early version called "The Green Lady," Steinbeck's hero fell in love with a forest, which he identified with his daughter (compare Barclay's love for his daughter April), and he died by walking as a sacrifice into the burning forest (the campfires of Barclay's followers set fire to the hillside, and Barclay purposely burned his hands dreadfully). Brand, Barclay, and Joseph Wayne are one kind of Faustian figure, the man who would be God.

To a God Unknown, like *Cup of Gold*, exhibits several themes and types of character that recur in later novels. We should notice, in particular, the feeble-minded Willy Romas, whose terrible dreams of a hard, barren country prefigured the drought. He is the first (except for Gertie in the *Stanford Spectator* story "Fingers of Cloud") of several imbeciles in Steinbeck's fiction (they appear in nine novels and two short stories). In some strange way the feeble-minded reveal to Steinbeck man's kinship with all creatures: he finds in them perceptions and intuitions which the intelligent often have not. Willy's dreams were truer to nature than Joseph's plans, revealing the cruelty and indifference of the Whole to men's designs. They were also oracular visions of myth. This novel is plainly a mythical narrative told in terms of a California farmer's struggle to build an enduring family community in a treacherous land, universalizing that struggle as man's relation to the universe.

3

⇜ THE PASTURES OF HEAVEN

IN *The Pastures of Heaven* (1932) Steinbeck has nearly attained full stature—and, it seems to me, the "nearly" can be dropped. Few copies were sold until Steinbeck's name meant something to the reading public; but were it not for the unpredictable vagaries of the book market, *The Pastures* instead of *Tortilla Flat* might have first established Steinbeck's reputation as an important novelist. The writing is simple, strong, objective, often moving, and the characterization is excellent. Both major and minor characters live and breathe, and for the first time we see one of Steinbeck's splendid animal characters: Lindo, the Lopez sisters' old horse, is delightful.

The Pastures of Heaven may be classified as either a novel or a collection of short stories strung together by a unifying device, like Sherwood Anderson's *Winesburg, Ohio*. In a short prologue we learn how the name Las Pasturas del Cielo was given to a little valley on the east side of the Santa Lucia Mountains near their northern tip (actually Corral de Tierra, a good way north of that valley in which Joseph Wayne settled). About 1776 a Spanish corporal, commanding a squad of cavalry in pursuit of runaway Indian workers, saw the valley from a ridge and, amazed at its beauty, said, "Here are the green pastures of Heaven to which our Lord leadeth us."

The story begins about 1928 when the Munroe family moved to the valley and took over the old Battle farm. The Battle farm was reputed to be under a curse; but although Bert Munroe had always been unlucky in his business ventures, he made his first success on the Battle farm. One night at T. B. Allen's general store he said, "I just happened to think, maybe my curse and the farm's curse got to fighting and killed each other off." Everybody laughed, and Allen, improving on the joke, said, "Maybe your curse and the farm's curse has mated and gone into a gopher hole like a pair of rattlesnakes. Maybe there'll be a lot of baby curses crawling around the Pastures the first thing we know." He spoke more truly than he realized. While Munroe prospered, misfortune came to other residents of the valley, always because of something that the Munroes did, though in no instance did the Munroes act with malice.

The curse is the unifying theme. The story of Shark Wicks, first to follow the introductory tale of the Battle farm, illustrates Steinbeck's device. Wicks made imaginary investments in stocks and bonds, keeping accounts of fancied purchases and sales in a big ledger. Since he often consulted his neighbors about investments, they believed that he was rich, although he had never had more than $500 at one time in his life. He had a beautiful but "incredibly stupid" daughter. He gloated over her beauty like a miser and carefully guarded her chastity. When the Munroes came to the valley, Wicks became excessively afraid of the adolescent Jimmie Munróe. Once when Wicks was away his wife and daughter went to a dance. Jimmie danced with Alice and kissed her. When Wicks heard about it he became enraged, seized a gun, and went towards the Munroe house, but was intercepted by a deputy sheriff. Bert Munroe put Wicks under bond to keep the peace, setting the amount at $10,000 because of Wicks's supposed wealth, and Wicks was forced to confess the humiliating truth.

If it is true that a Munroe act precipitated the change of fortune in each story, to what degree were the Munroes culpable? Critics interpret the Munroes according to Steinbeck's original intention, as expressed in a letter to his agents: he wanted, he said, to show how the happiness and harmony of the twenty families who lived in the valley were destroyed by a family of newcomers, who committed no intentionally malicious acts, and yet, as if surrounded by an evil cloud, brought injury to everyone with whom they had dealings. Something like this had really happened in Corral de Tierra. Yet, according to Lewis Gannett, the book turned out somewhat differently; as always, he says, Steinbeck learned much about his stories and characters in the process of creating them. And in the novel as written, the Munroe role is not so easily interpreted as Steinbeck's early statement would indicate. As Hildegard Schumann points out,

John Steinbeck

Steinbeck's own attitude to the curse, i.e., the Munroe acts, remains unclear in the finished book.

Only in the story of Raymond Banks can a Munroe be said to be truly at fault. Raymond, owner of a large chicken ranch, liked to visit his friend, warden of San Quentin prison, and witness a hanging; for him it was a kind of religious experience. Bert Munroe was both horrified and fascinated when he heard about Banks's favorite recreation. One day he asked Banks to get him an invitation to witness a hanging. When Banks did so, Bert backed out, explaining that as a boy he had seen a cripple horribly botch a job of killing a chicken; and he imagined that executioners could likewise botch a hanging, causing terrible agonies to the condemned. In the ensuing argument he said to Banks, "If you had any imagination, you'd see for yourself, and you wouldn't go up to see some poor devil get killed." In consequence Banks lost his appetite for attending hangings. So by asking Banks for an invitation, then turning it down, and then finding fault with Banks, Munroe deliberately acted in such a way as to affect Banks's behavior. Only here is there a trace of malice in a Munroe act.

In the story of Junius Maltby the Munroe act led directly to Maltby's decision to leave the valley and go back to work in the city. In this case the Munroes intended to be charitable; when Mrs. Munroe saw the ragged Robbie Maltby, she gave him some new clothes. In all other stories the change of fortune arises from an accidental or totally innocent act of the Munroes, and to blame them for subsequent events strains the evidence (this is true, I believe, of the Lopez story, too, in which Bert's jest had serious consequences). T. B. Allen's joking remark, made to Shark Wicks, about Jimmie and Alice led more directly than Jimmie's act to "disaster," and the true agent of Shark's downfall was Shark himself, overvaluing his daughter's beauty and neurotically obsessed with her chastity. Molly Morgan, the schoolteacher, encouraging Tularecito, the gnomelike halfwit, to look for gnomes and elves, precipitated the chain of events that led to Tularecito's commitment to a mental institution. In the story of Pat Humbert, the Munroes cannot be blamed because Pat overheard Mae Munroe admire a Banksia rose on the front of his house and express a wish to see the interior, because the house looked like a Vermont house. These remarks caused Pat to make the interior over in Vermont style and to think of marrying Mae—but he told nobody and found out too late that Mae would soon marry another. The tragedy lies in Pat's character and past.

22

Mrs. E. G. Ainsworth and Elizabeth Otis

JOHN STEINBECK AND HIS SISTER, ESTHER

John Steinbeck

We can say only that the Munroes were agents of the curse, which means no more than the coincidence that they were involved to some degree in every change of fortune. Now we must consider another question, whether these changes were in every instance a change from better to worse, as critics generally assume. In the story of Junius Maltby the change may be looked at either way. Junius, an accountant, went to the Pastures for his health and married the widow with whom he boarded. Junius was a lazy fellow: he would go out to work on his wife's farm, but would inevitably drift away to sit by a stream and read, usually Stevenson, his favorite author. The farm rapidly went to ruin. Mrs. Maltby died, leaving Junius with an infant son, Robert Louis. Somehow the boy survived. Father, son, and hired man (who soon became as lazy as Junius), ragged and unkempt, spent their time reading and talking. "They didn't make conversation; rather they let a seedling of thought sprout by itself, and then watched with wonder while it sent out branching limbs." Finally Robbie had to go to school. Despite his rags he became a leader on the playground because of his vivid imagination and skill in inventing games. His schoolmates visited the Maltby farm on Saturdays and listened to Junius read *Treasure Island* and talk about all sorts of marvelous things. It was an idyllic existence, as Steinbeck presents it, although the Maltbys sometimes went hungry when they couldn't find eggs or cucumbers in the tangled growth on the farm. Junius' neighbors condemned him for his sloth and "outlawed him from decent society." Junius, however, "knew nothing about the dislike of his neighbors. He was still gloriously happy. His life was as unreal, as romantic and as unimportant as his thinking." Then the Munroes offered new clothes to Robbie; Bert talked to Junius, who for the first time realized "what people were saying about us." "I didn't know," he said, "I was doing an injury to the boy." So with a feeling of shame he and Robbie, dressed in cheap suits, left the valley for San Francisco, where Junius intended to resume work as an accountant.

Some readers may applaud this outcome, believing that work and responsibility are better than indolence, irresponsibility, and the neighbors' contempt. But Steinbeck apparently did not see it that way. In the postscript to the separate publication of the Maltby story, *Nothing So Monstrous*, he imagines that Junius and Robbie returned to the Pastures, occupied a cave in the outlying wilderness, and resumed their old way of life: "I don't know that this is true. I only hope to God it is."

In other instances we may say, if we wish, that residents of the

24

Pastures suffered a change for the worse in that Munroe interference upset their designs for living. We must also look at the moral and psychic effects of the changes. The fate of Shark Wicks is significant. He had built up a private world of make-believe based on his daughter's beauty and his ledger of fictitious stock transactions. The catastrophe was painful, but it was a moment of truth. Afterwards Shark's wife convinced him that he really could make money if he tried, and so he decided to sell his farm, go elsewhere, and prove himself. We don't know how successful he will be, and it doesn't matter: what matters is that he will act in a real world. Shark did know something about investments; even if we allow for a little *post eventum* juggling, he would have made money if his imaginary investments had been real.

The pattern of catastrophe illustrated in the Wicks story is present, I believe, in every other. In each the principal character had founded his tranquil life in the valley upon an unhealthy adjustment, an evasion of reality, an illusion, or an unrealizable dream; and a deed of a Munroe forced him to face the truth, if but for a moment. Pat Humbert, Helen Van Deventer, and Molly Morgan refused to surrender their private worlds. But the Lopez sisters faced the truth that they really were what they pretended not to be, prostitutes; they had not literally taken "the money of shame," but had given themselves to customers who bought three or more enchiladas. John Whiteside, as a successful farmer and community leader, is the only character who is not neurotic, deluded, or grotesque. He nursed not an illusion but a dream, inherited from his father, Richard, of a large Whiteside family living in the big house which Richard built in the Pastures— not an impossible dream, had fortune favored the Whitesides. But single son was followed by single son, and John's son, Bill, destroyed the Whiteside dream when he married Mae Munroe and moved to Monterey. Bill's rejection of the Whiteside design was foreshadowed in his failure to listen when, in Bill's boyhood, his father read to him from Herodotus, Thucydides and Xenophon; for Richard had read to the delighted John from the Greek historians, and thus made them symbols of the Whiteside tradition.

The impersonal operation of the curse, as expressed in the varying effect of the Munroe actions, is brought out in the order of the stories, which are linked in a series of ironic contrasts. (1) Bert Munroe failed in business before coming to the Pastures; there he became a successful farmer. Shark Wicks, not prospering as a farmer in the Pastures, left the valley to make money in business. (2) Alice Wicks was beautiful and stupid; Tularecito was ugly and stupid. Alice had no talents; Tularecito had a strange skill. Nobody adequately realized Alice's limitations; everybody was aware of Tularecito's. (3) Tularecito searched for the little people, because they were his own people, but never found them; Hilda Van Deventer saw them in dreams and visions without wanting to, since they tormented her. Tularecito, not insane, was committed to a mental hospital; Hilda, quite mad, was never committed. (4) Helen Van Deventer lost her husband just before her daughter was born and worked hard at rearing an insane child with final defeat. Junius Maltby lost his wife when his son was born, and without any effort reared a normal child. (5) Junius Maltby, leading a lazy but moral life, left the Pastures to take an honorable occupation in the city. The Lopez sisters, leading an industrious but immoral life, left the valley to follow a dishonorable occupation in the city. (6) The Lopez sisters, not respected in the Pastures, left the valley to give up their make-believe and accept reality. Molly Morgan, much respected in the Pastures, left the valley to keep up her make-believe. (7) Molly Morgan, an imaginative person, pleaded sickness and suddenly gave up a position that she liked, because she did not want to identify herself with a suffering man. Raymond Banks, an unimaginative person, pleaded sickness and suddenly gave up a custom that he liked, because he had identified himself with suffering men. (8) Raymond Banks, a gregarious man who enjoyed the company of others, liked the sight of death; when he realized what dying meant, he turned away from death. Pat Humbert, a lonely man who sought others' company compulsively, hated the dead and enjoyed the sight of life; but on the point of realizing life, he turned away from it. (9) Pat Humbert, uneducated and without family feeling, built a Vermont house for a particular woman and abandoned it when he failed to get her. Richard Whiteside, educated and endowed with strong family feeling, built a New England house for a wife before he had a particular woman in mind, and both he and his son continued to live in the house after their hopes of abundant progeny were disappointed.

Thus the curse affected every resident, whatever his virtues, faults, or condition. As the principal unifying device, the curse is the central mythical construct of *The Pastures*. It is also the oracle of this novel, serving much the same purpose as Merlin's and Gwenliana's prophecies in *Cup of Gold,* and as John Wayne's blessing and dying prediction, the paisanos' prophecy of dry years, and Willy Romas' dreams in *To a God Unknown*. In each case, the oracular statement has a paradigmatic or programmatic purpose, sketching in brief general terms the course and outcome of the action. In *The Pastures* the comprehensive oracle, expressed in the curse, runs counter to individual oracles of particular stories. For example, when Richard Whiteside came to the Pastures, he looked for an omen and found it in a flurry of oak leaves blown toward the valley. This omen is part of the particular myth which underlies the Whiteside story, a legend of Greek colonization, a kind of tale frequent in Greek mythographers and historians, especially in Herodotus, whose history Richard read often. Richard "remembered the colonists from Athens and from Lacedaemon looking for new lands described by vague oracles; he thought of the Aztecs plodding forward after their guiding eagle." Like an ancient city-founder he looked to the sky to find some sign from birds or clouds. Then the oak leaves spoke to him, as if from Zeus's oak at Dodona. He was delighted: "Many a fine city was founded because of a hint from the gods no more broad than that." But Steinbeck inverts the myth. The founder failed: a contrary force was at work.

The story of Tularecito is built upon folktales of changelings. Pancho, the Mexican Indian who found the infant, was always sure that Tularecito was one of the little people. When he found the child, as he told the story, "the baby winked maliciously and said in a deep voice, 'Look! I have very sharp teeth.' " Tularecito looked like a gnome, and his appearance gave him his name, Little Frog (possibly Steinbeck had Kipling's Mowgli in mind, too). He had strange skills and a man's strength at the age of six. When Molly Morgan read stories about gnomes and elves to her class, Tularecito at once realized that these were his own people, and with Molly's encouragement went to look for them. Herein the folktale is reversed: a changeling does not want his true nature discovered; but Tularecito wanted to quit mankind and go home. "My father, I have come home," he called, but he could not find the little people; they were not there, despite Miss Morgan's words. Here is the pathos of Tularecito's story. His search took him to the Munroe orchard and to the Napa asylum.

Molly Morgan's story exploits the theme soon to be used in *Tortilla Flat,* the ne'er-do-well as chivalric figure. Molly thought of her father as a knight or Robin Hood. One day she walked to an old cabin associated with the bandit Vasquez, to whom, as to his more famous contemporary, Joaquin Murrieta, California lore soon assigned numerous cabins, caves, and rendezvous. Molly imagined that "Vasquez had her father's gay face, his shining eyes." The author of *Cup of Gold* pur-

27

posely gave her father the name Morgan (in the shift from knight-errant to Robin Hood, Molly romanticized her father's weaknesses). Bill Whiteside was the unimaginative spokesman of reality, pointing out that Vasquez was a thief and murderer, and so Bill spoiled Molly's day, as later Bert Munroe's talk about his alcoholic hired man threatened to spoil Molly's illusions about her father (contrived illusions, one notices).

Shark Wicks was a Faust who created riches out of paper and a Helen out of inert material; he is not Peer Gynt or Brand, but Jonson's Subtle the Alchemist. The Pat Humbert story is indebted to tales of haunted houses, as is the introductory story of the Battle farm. When Pat cleared out the old furniture and burned it, he was engaged in exorcism: "The table and chairs cracked as they released their ghosts into the fire." In the end he merely replaced two old ghosts with younger phantoms, "two puzzled spirits," whereas Bert Munroe, remodeling the Battle house, successfully routed all ghosts.

The curse theme is the string upon which the particular myths are strung like beads. The necklace is boxed within the myth of earthly paradise, expressed in title, prologue, and epilogue. In the prologue a Spanish corporal saw the valley, named it, and dreamed of retiring there to end his days in peace; but he died of the pox in an old barn near the mission. In the epilogue a bus with a motley group of passengers stopped on the ridge above the valley at sunset and looked down upon the farms, gardens, fields, and groves. "No poverty there, no smells, no trouble," said the priest; and every passenger thought that if he could live down there, he would be happy and at peace. A prosperous man predicted rich men's houses and golf links—a final oracle of suburban development which suits the whole thesis, a realtor's vision of earthly paradise, realistic and realizable. The real world, the Munroe family, was bound to break in. The valley had a kind of idyllic charm before the Munroes came, but it was a paradise built on illusions, neuroses, evasions—an unstable Eden.

The Eden idea is symbolized in gardens and orchards: George Battle's carefully tended vegetable garden; Helen Van Deventer's newly made lawn and garden of cinerarias under oaks with lobelia borders beside the walks; Raymond Banks's model chicken ranch, where chickens were killed in primeval innocence; and the wild growth of the Maltby farm, which fed its inhabitants (usually) without tillage. Junius, Jakob, and Robbie talked about "where Atlantis lay"; Junius pointed out that the lovely horses of the Parthenon frieze were "bound for a celestial pasture." On the day when Molly

28

Morgan visited, the fine talk ended "when the dour Jakob opposed his [Junius'] idea of the eviction from the Garden of Eden." Soon after that, the Maltbys left their Eden for San Francisco.

Reality defeats the dream. Steinbeck translates myth and legend into twentieth-century realism, showing what paradise, curses, oracles, ghosts, knights, Robin Hoods, and gnomes amount to in everyday terms. Myth is used ironically, as in *Cup of Gold*, but *The Pastures* lacks the cynical touch of the earlier novel. Here the myth not only is set in contrast to reality, but also serves to sublimate reality, making us aware that ordinary people are interesting.

The Novels of Steinbeck

4

~§ TORTILLA FLAT

STEINBECK has loved no town so much as Monterey. It has been
his town in a way that Salinas, Pacific Grove, and New York have
not. It has an old-world flavor that has lingered from the days when
it was the seat of Spanish and Mexican governments. The Steinbeck
Monterey, which is not necessarily the same thing as the real Monterey, fights a losing battle against twentieth-century civilization, but
has not yet gone under.

Monterey sits on the slope of a hill, with a blue bay below it and
with a forest of tall dark pine trees at its back. The lower parts of the
town are inhabited by Americans, Italians, catchers and canners of
fish. But on the hill where the forest and the town intermingle, where
the streets are innocent of asphalt and the corners free of street lights,
the old inhabitants of Monterey are embattled as the Ancient Britons
are embattled in Wales. These are the paisanos.

This purlieu is Tortilla Flat, a purely fictitious subcommunity of
Steinbeck's Monterey which represents the town's paisano population.
"What is a paisano? He is a mixture of Spanish, Indian, Mexican
and assorted Caucasian bloods. His ancestors have lived in California
for a hundred or two years."

The paisanos are a people to whom Steinbeck is sympathetic.
Paisano characters had appeared in *To a God Unknown* and in short
stories later to be collected in *The Long Valley*. Steinbeck himself
knew paisanos, talked and drank with them, listened to their tales,

and some paisano lore, Moore says, he learned from Susan Gregory, a resident of Monterey, to whom *Tortilla Flat* is dedicated. He put these people into a novel which has delighted many readers, but the book's unexpected popularity had its disconcerting features: readers liked the paisanos for wrong reasons, for being quaint curiosities, contrary to Steinbeck's intention.

Tortilla Flat at first sight appears to have a loose construction like *The Pastures of Heaven,* several stories set within a frame and written about the same people. It is, in fact, much more tightly constructed. Every story has the same central characters, Danny and his friends; we do not move from one family to another as in *The Pastures.* And it has a perceptible plot with a gradual rise and a swifter fall.

Danny, returning from the war, found that he had inherited two houses in Tortilla Flat. He rented one to Pilon, who never had money to pay rent. Pablo Sanchez and Jesus Maria Corcoran moved in with Pilon, but they never had money either. Relations between Danny and Pilon were becoming strained when Pilon's house burned down. Then the three friends moved in with Danny. The four admitted the Pirate, a half-witted man, and his five dogs to the house, hoping to get the Pirate's hoard of money; and he did bring a big bag of quarters to them for safekeeping, explaining that he had vowed a golden candlestick, worth a thousand quarters, to Saint Francis for the recovery of a dog. The friends were loyal to their trust, and the bag of quarters became "the symbolic center of the friendship." Soon afterwards Joe Portagee joined the group and stole the Pirate's bag. His housemates gave him a beating and, recovering most of the money, found that the Pirate had enough to buy his candle. Several adventures occurred before and after the fulfilment of the vow; but finally the good days of the fellowship came to an end. Danny deserted his friends and ran wild; when he came back, he was listless and melancholy. To rekindle his spirits his friends gave a big party, which all Tortilla Flat attended. Danny had a last uproarious fling, surpassing all his past exploits of drinking, wenching, and fighting, until he ran outside to fight "The Enemy who is worthy of Danny," fell into a gulch, and was killed. The evening after the funeral his house burned down and the friends scattered.

It is a picaresque novel: Danny and his friends are pleasant rogues who never work unless extremity drives them to it. They pick up food, drink, and fun as chance offers, thinking nothing of petty theft, prevarication, and trickery, and they get along quite well without running water, electric lights, and a change of clothes. They live for the pleasures of the passing day: all they want is enough to eat, plenty of red wine, a cozy place to sit and talk, an occasional amour or brawl. "Love and fighting, and a little wine," said Pilon, "Then you are always young, always happy." They use money and barterable goods mainly for buying wine or presents for women. Although they literally break the law often enough, they are not criminals. Nor do they lack conscience and moral feelings (except perhaps Joe Portagee). Still, they are hardly paragons of virtue and reliability, and he who puts his trust in them is likely to regret it. We may give them credit for keeping faith with the Pirate and keeping his bag of quarters inviolate; yet we should remember that the Pirate's quarters were devoted to Saint Francis, and also that Danny's second house burned down because Pablo, having bought a candle for Saint Francis, had used it profanely instead. "Have you forgotten that this candle was blessed? . . . Here is the principle which takes the waxen rod outside the jurisdiction of physics." Danny and his friends could not risk offending the saint again: they had but one house left.

The paisanos are great moralizers, but their moralizing too often consists in finding noble reasons for satisfying desires at a friend's expense, as when Pilon took Joe's serge trousers. Wanting wine as he sat beside the sleeping Joe on the beach, Pilon pretended to himself that he wanted it for Joe. Searching his own and Joe's pockets for money or some exchangeable object and finding none, he noticed Joe's serge pants. Now Joe's friends wore jeans; the trousers were much too small for Joe anyway, and besides Joe had stolen a blanket from Danny's house and needed punishment. So off came the trousers, which Pilon exchanged for a quart of wine (having asked for a gallon). Drinking the quart at once, he then "thought sadly of his friend out there on the beach," liable to arrest for indecent exposure, because a harpy (Mrs. Torrelli) "had tried to buy Pilon's friend's pants for a miserable quart of miserable wine." As he left Torrelli's he recovered the trousers and, posing as Joe's benefactor, returned them to the awakened and embarrassed Joe.

This is the sort of picaresque episode which has caused many readers to enjoy *Tortilla Flat* as an entertaining account of amiable rascals. The book, however, is a good deal more than a picaresque novel, and we have not said all that there is to say about its characters when we have called them rogues. As "good people of laughter and kindness" Steinbeck sets them in contrast to the commercial civilization that surrounds them; they "are clean of commercialism, free of the complicated systems of American business." This is a recurring theme of Steinbeck's fiction: the values of a simple people are opposed, as more healthy and viable, to the values of a competitive society.

That income property may damage human relations is an important thesis of *Tortilla Flat*. When Danny told Pilon that he had inherited two houses, Pilon said, "Now the great times are done. . . . Thou art lifted above thy friends. Thou art a man of property." The final phrase, one feels, is deliberately reminiscent of Galsworthy's Soames Forsyte, the man of property who got income from rented houses. The ownership of a rented house did adversely affect Danny's friendship with Pilon, and so when that house burned, Danny gladly gave up the status of rentier, saying, "Now we can be free and happy again." But Danny still owned one house; it was still true that as a houseowner he could no longer smash windows at will or joyously destroy property with a clear conscience. "Always the weight of the house was upon him; always the responsibility to his friends." So he fled, and that was the beginning of the end.

The house was the body of an organism. In *Tortilla Flat* Steinbeck's biological point of view becomes explicit, and for the first time he makes deliberate, if humorous, use of the conception of the group as organism. The first words are:

> This is the story of Danny and of Danny's friends and of Danny's house. It is a story of how these three became one thing, so that in Tortilla Flat if you speak of Danny's house you do not mean a structure of wood flaked with old whitewash, . . . No, when you speak of Danny's house you are understood to mean a unit of which the parts are men, from which came sweetness and joy, philanthropy and, in the end, a mystic sorrow.

The group organism is more than just the sum of its parts, and the emotions of its unit parts coalesce into a single group emotion. When the friends discovered Joe Portagee's theft of the Pirate's money, they waited in the house for his return: "No words were spoken, but a wave of cold fury washed and crouched in the room. The feeling in the house was the feeling of a rock when the fuse is burning in toward the dynamite." So *Tortilla Flat* is on one level the life history of an organism, which was conceived when Danny, just out of jail, met Pilon and told him about the two houses. When Pilon, Pablo, and Jesus Maria moved in with Danny, the organism was born. It grew (when the Pirate and Joe Portagee came in), thrived for a time, had

33

good and bad experiences, became sick, and died; and the burning of the house was the cremation of the organism's body.

Just as individual organisms are units of a group organism, so smaller group organisms may be units of larger group organisms. Danny's household was part of Tortilla Flat, and Tortilla Flat was part of Monterey. Tortilla Flat as a whole had qualities like those of Danny's fellowship, but other qualities too, since each paisano household had its peculiarities. In Monterey as a whole paisano characteristics mingle with other kinds; yet Monterey is in certain respects like Danny's house: "There is a changeless quality about Monterey. . . . On Tortilla Flat, above Monterey, the routine is changeless, too; . . . In Danny's house there was even less change." Monterey too can behave like a single organism: "All Monterey began to make gradual instinctive preparations against the night"; then Steinbeck reports the unvarying acts of several persons and creatures at this time of day, not as acts of autonomous individuals, but as coordinated movements of a single organism's parts. The group organism has a nervous system, the pathways of rumor, which carries information and emotions through the whole collective body. In several books Steinbeck expresses his wonder at the uncanny speed and operation of rumor, as in *Tortilla Flat:* "One evening, by that quick and accurate telegraph no one understands, news came in that a coast guard cutter had gone on the rocks near Carmel." Again, when Danny's friends began to plan the final party, the rumor of it flew about Tortilla Flat and beyond into Monterey: "The morning was electric with the news."

This organismic complex—Danny, Danny's fellowship, Tortilla Flat, Monterey—is doomed to defeat before the forces of twentieth-century civilization. Monterey becomes just another American city, and Tortilla Flat fades away into it. The old organism was changeless—that was its *hamartia*—and lacked the resilience and vigor needed for resistance. It was too easily infected by the insidious pride of property ownership.

The organismic complex may also be seen as an ecological community, for Steinbeck's interest in ecology first makes itself plainly felt in *Tortilla Flat*. The paisanos illustrate the ecological principle that every niche in the environment is likely to be filled and that some kind of creature will adapt itself to every possible source of subsistence. In his later Foreword, Steinbeck says that the paisanos are "people who merge successfully with their habitat. In men this is called philosophy, and it is a fine thing." The Pirate brought his friends scraps and leftovers collected at the back doors of restaurants, very good fare sometimes, "fresh fish, half pies, untouched loaves of stale bread, meat that required only a little soda to take the green out"; once he had "a steak out of which only a little was missing." After the Pirate had bought his votive candlestick, he spent his daily quarter, earned by selling kindling wood, for food, which he brought to the house. Sometimes the friends threw rocks at fishing boats from the wharf and picked up the fish thrown back at them. They also pilfered food from restaurants and stores and got wine in devious ways. Some paisanos gleaned the bean fields. We perceive, therefore, that the paisanos, particularly of Danny's kind, are symbiotics or commensals (some would say parasites) of the Monterey community, depending upon others for their food, living on the pickings. So in one aspect *Tortilla Flat* is the story of this symbiosis. The paisanos, trying to preserve their own values, pushed into a corner of the habitat, are forced to become scavengers and jackal-like snatchers of others' food.

But more important than the organismic and ecological themes, though merging with them, is the Arthurian theme; for the Arthur story, as Steinbeck has said plainly, provided *Tortilla Flat* its central structure. On the first page Steinbeck says,

> For Danny's house was not unlike the Round Table, and Danny's friends were not unlike the knights of it. And this is the story of how that group came into being, of how it flourished and grew to be an organization beautiful and wise. This story deals with the adventuring of Danny's friends, with the good they did, with their thoughts and their endeavors. In the end, this story tells how the talisman was lost and how the group disintegrated.

This broad hint was ignored by readers of the manuscript and by reviewers of the published book. The failure of publishers' readers to recognize the Arthurian theme puzzled Steinbeck. In a letter to his agents, early in 1934, he said,

> "I had expected that the plan of the Arthurian cycle would be recognized, that my Gawaine and Launcelot that my Arthur and Galahad would be recognized. Even the incident of the Sangreal in the search of the forest is not clear enough I guess. The form is that of the Malory version, the coming of Arthur and the mystic quality of owning a house, the forming of the round table, the adventures of the knights and finally, the mystic adventures of Danny. However, I seem not to have made any of this clear."

When the book appeared in 1935 Steinbeck had provided it with chapter headings in the style of Caxton's Malory: e.g., Chapter 1, "How Danny, home from the wars, found himself an heir, and how he swore to protect the helpless."

As recently as 1957 Steinbeck said that *Tortilla Flat* was deliberately based on Malory's book. An author's own statement of his structural plan should be of prime importance for the study and interpretation of a book. Yet in dealing with *Tortilla Flat* critics usually brush aside the Arthurian theme with the remark that there is nothing more to say about it than what Steinbeck himself has said, that the structural similarities which Steinbeck mentioned are so general as to lack significance, and that it is vain to look for detailed parallels. Of course, one must not look for one-to-one correspondences throughout; and if we say, truly enough, that Danny corresponds to Arthur and Pilon to Launcelot (Pablo seems to be Gawaine and Jesus Maria to be Galahad), we need not suppose that Danny is always Arthur, Pilon always Launcelot. This is to misconceive a creative writer's use of a mythical theme. Faulkner's *A Fable* illustrates nicely what a writer does with a myth: the old French Marshal is now God the Father, now Satan, and again Pontius Pilate; the Messiah is married to Mary Magdalene. In taking the Arthurian ingredient of *Tortilla Flat* seriously one is not reading the work as a modern version of the Arthur legend, since obviously the novel is not an Arthurian legend, any more than Faulkner's novel is the gospel story. The structural plan of Malory's *Arthur* had to be condensed for use as model for *Tortilla Flat*, and one rescue of a maid in distress will do for twenty. But Malory's Arthur story did in fact determine the narrative sequence and pervade the whole content.

First notice the narrative sequence. Arthur [Danny] after an obscure boyhood unexpectedly inherited a kingdom [house] and was transformed from ordinary manhood to heaven's viceroy as lord of the land [a landlord who experienced "the mystic quality of owning a house"]. The new king had trouble with subject kings and barons [Pilon, Pablo], who refused to pay homage [rent], but were finally defeated [the rented house burned down] and reconciled. Arthur [Danny], chastened by experience of rule, gathered knights [friends] to his Round Table [house] and gave them lands [shelter and a place to sleep]. The knights swore an oath of devotion and fealty [Danny's friends promised to see that Danny should never go hungry]. Arthur and his knights gave their attention to Pelles, the Maimed King, and the Grail which he kept [Pirate and his treasure].

Percival, undervalued by the knights (a simpleton in the pre-Malory legend), was placed among humble knights [the Pirate was given a corner of Danny's house, where he slept among his dogs]. The knights (but not Arthur) set out in search of the Grail for the welfare of Arthur's kingdom [the friends, without Danny, searched on Saint Andrew's Eve for mystic treasure for Danny's welfare]. Launcelot [Pilon, who said, "It is because my heart is clean of selfishness that I can find this treasure"] achieved a vision of the Grail [a phosphorescent light above the spot], but failed in the quest [found a Geodetic Survey marker]. Demon women [Sweets Ramirez] tempted Percival and Bors [Danny], who were finally saved from their machinations (the partly successful efforts of Launcelot's friends to draw him away from Guinevere, a later episode in Malory, are merged with the demon women's temptations in the successful effort of Danny's friends to separate him from Sweets). An old man came to Arthur's court with the boy Galahad [a Mexican corporal came to Danny's house with his infant son], who would be greater than his father [as the corporal intended his son to be]. Then the Grail appeared to the knights at supper and supplied them with meat and drink [Danny and his friends "were sitting in the living room, waiting for the daily miracle of food"; soon the Pirate (keeper of the true Grail) came in with a bag of mackerels]. Arthur and his knights, finishing their supper, went to look at the Siege Perilous, where Galahad sat [after their meal Danny and his friends went to look at the corporal's son lying in an apple box]. Galahad did not live long [the child died]. Percival [Joe Portagee] came upon a damsel [Tia Ignacia] who gave him wine to drink; he fell asleep in her pavilion [chair] and afterwards made love to her (here Joe with his ill-fitting trousers is also La Cote Male Taile, whom a lady first scorned and then loved). Percival, Galahad, and Bors achieved the quest of the Grail [the friends' true treasure was the Pirate's bag of quarters, "the symbolic center of the friendship, the point of trust about which the fraternity revolved" (and the Pirate kept the house supplied with food, as the Grail provided often for the Round Table)].

After the quest the Round Table knights reassembled [the friends became reconciled with Joe Portagee], Launcelot saved Guinevere from death and again from capture [the friends rescued Teresina Cortez in the bean shortage] and had amorous trysts with her [Teresina found herself pregnant again]. The knights, as formerly, enjoyed tournaments and the fellowship of the Round Table ["Of the good life at Danny's House" (Chapter XIV)], until Arthur be-

37

came Launcelot's enemy. Arthur left England to fight elsewhere [Danny left the house and took to fighting elsewhere]. In Arthur's absence Mordred claimed the throne, relying upon the regency which Arthur had granted him and upon forged letters [Torrelli, carrying a deed signed by Danny, claimed ownership of the house]. Arthur's loyal subjects opposed Mordred's claim [Danny's friends foiled Torrelli's attempt to occupy the house]. Arthur returned to England [Danny came back to the house] and in a great last battle defeated his enemies [at the final big party "roaring battles . . . raged through whole clots of men," and "Danny defied and attacked the whole party," prevailing over everybody], but mortally wounded, went off over a lake to Avalon with supernatural companions [Danny, going outside to fight The Enemy, met him and fell into a gulch to his death]. None of Arthur's knights [Danny's friends] was present at his funeral and burial.

The parallels, of course, should not be more obvious than they are. Steinbeck started with tales, true and legendary, about paisanos. He perceived something in paisano behavior that reminded him of Arthur's knights, far-fetched as any similarity may seem offhand, and he believed the likeness worth developing. The manner in which he could assimilate paisano deeds and habits to knightly ways is perhaps even better revealed in narrative details than in the more general structural parallels.

Like the knights of old, Danny, Pilon, and Joe Portagee were warriors, having enlisted in the American army in the First World War. And Danny, like every knight, was a horseman: "At twenty-five his legs were bent to the exact curves of a horse's sides," and few men could handle mules as well. Danny's company liked fights with one another or with anybody: Arthur's knights loved jousts and hostile encounters on the road. Both paisanos and knights fought over women, who were likely to favor the victor. Danny and Pilon had "a really fine fight" in the presence of two girls, who "kicked whichever man happened to be down." The knights' ladies were sometimes like that too. It hardly mattered to a certain damsel whether Palomides or Corsabrin won their fight, for she was ready to go with either (Malory 10:47). Another cheerfully spent the night with Epinogris after he had killed her father and a companion knight; the next morning she went off with Helior when he wounded Epinogris; later Palomides restored her to Epinogris (Malory 10:83). Sometimes several knights attacked one man and took his lady from him; likewise several soldiers twice took the hardly reluctant Arabella Gross

38

from Jesus Maria, and the second time Arabella helped them beat him up. Nor for all their chivalrous talk were Arthur's knights less lecherous than the paisanos. Arthur himself had amorous relations with Lyonors and Lot's wife Margawse, Launcelot with Guinevere and Elaine, Tristram with Isoud, Gawaine with Ettard. Moreover, the knights enjoyed good food and wine quite as much as did Danny and his friends.

Tortilla Flat has the same Catholic background as Malory's *Arthur*. In both books references to Masses, rituals, and sacred objects are frequent; the characters in both speak as men to whom the Faith is second nature. Miracles occur, visions are seen, in Tortilla Flat as in the kingdom of Logres. The Pirate's dogs saw a vision of Saint Francis—so the Pirate believed—and he almost saw it too. As Jesus Maria lay on the beach near Seaside, the waves washed an empty rowboat ashore. He rowed it to Monterey, sold it for seven dollars, and bought both wine and a gift for Arabella. "God floated the little rowboat to you," said Pilon; and God sent a self-moving boat to Jesus Maria's Arthurian counterpart, Galahad, who on boarding it found a silk crown and a marvelous sword. Another time an empty boat came to Arthur as he stood on a riverbank, and carried him to a castle where he was served with wines and meats.

Danny's bed was the Siege Perilous. When Big Joe tried to lie in it, a stick came down hard on the soles of his feet "so that even he learned the inviolable quality of Danny's bed." Pilon taking the sleeping Joe's trousers and going off in search of wine is Launcelot taking the sleeping Kay's armor and going off in search of adventure (Malory 6:11). Even the paisanos' habit of sleeping in the open likens them to the knights, who often lay down in a forest or by a well; and as harts and deer crossed the knights' paths, so chickens crossed the paths of Danny and his friends. Danny in Monterey jail is Arthur imprisoned in Sir Damas' castle. Petey Ravanno at last won Gracie Montez' love when he tried suicide: Ettard finally loved Pelleas when she thought him dead. Old Man Ravanno, lovesick over a girl, is like Merlin besotted over Nineve; and as Merlin, entering a rock at Nineve's request, was shut therein and died, so when old Ravanno entered a tool house to win Tonia's love by feigning suicide, the door slammed shut, nobody saw him, and he really hanged himself. In many details like these, the paisanos show their kinship with Arthur's knights. They even use the same kind of speech: in courteous expression, statements of moral sentiment, accepted codes of conduct, even in their hypocrisy and insincerity, the paisanos resemble the knights. The use of the familiar second person and the literal translation of Spanish expressions into English have the effect of giving the paisanos a speech like that of Malory's knights.

Having observed the pervasive Arthurian tone of *Tortilla Flat*, we can no longer deny significance to Steinbeck's own statements about his debt to Malory. But how does the Arthurian reading of *Tortilla Flat* harmonize with the organismic and ecological reading? The Round Table, of course, was a group, a community, and therefore a social organism. There may appear to be a great gap between the nobility of the Arthurian cycle and the squalor of the meaner sort of commensal organism. However, it is just this contrast that gives *Tortilla Flat* much of its picaresque quality. And it has a deeper meaning too, a meaning like that of Mark Twain's *A Connecticut Yankee in King Arthur's Court*. After all, the knights were no more industrious and productive than Danny's band: the fact is that they too lived on the products of others' labor. In reading Malory we are now and then reminded that lands which other men tilled gave the knights their living. If these amiable and idle paisanos are parasites, so were the knights. If the knights were courteous men, so are the paisanos.

But the term "mock-heroic" seems misleading if applied to *Tortilla Flat*. Steinbeck is too fond of both paisanos and Arthurian legend to be guilty of belittling either. *Tortilla Flat* both illuminates the Dark Ages and dignifies the paisanos. We are again confronted with an antithesis: the actual lives of men who enjoy fighting, live on others' labor, and shun work are opposed to the legendary lives of men whose mode of life was much the same. If anything, the paisanos are more amusing and less dangerous than the knights. The sort of thing that they do is the stuff that legends are made of, as Steinbeck tells us in his Preface:

> It is well that this cycle be put down on paper so that in a future time scholars, hearing the legends, may not say as they say of Arthur and of Roland and of Robin Hood—"There was no Danny nor any group of Danny's friends, nor any house. Danny is a nature god and his friends primitive symbols of the wind, the sky, the sun."

This quotation may be called the primary oracle of *Tortilla Flat;* for again Steinbeck hints at the pagan myth behind Arthurian legend: Danny is the sun that rises, rules the sky and the wind, has his high noon and brilliant afternoon, and then sets into darkness.

The burning of the house is the glory of the sunset—we should notice that in Steinbeck's first five novels (including *In Dubious Battle*) a fire or parching drought (which was a fire in an early draft of *To a God Unknown*) occurs either at the climax or at the conclusion. Notice the portents which posterity will attribute to the great climactic party: "It must be remembered . . . that Danny is now a god. . . . In twenty years it may be plainly remembered that the clouds flamed and spelled DANNY in tremendous letters; that the moon dripped blood; that the wolf of the world bayed prophetically from the mountains of the Milky Way." Thus Steinbeck resumes his opening jest. We are not expected to take Danny's divinity seriously, and yet Steinbeck tells us how gods and heroes are made.

Tortilla Flat thus mingles seriousness with jest, enjoyment with deeper meanings. Its tone blends humor, bittersweet pathos, and the objectivity of a sympathetic and amused narrator of legendary events in a language just different enough from ordinary speech to be distinctive and to place the narrative at one remove from the commonplace. Again and again the reader encounters expressions both surprising and delightful, as Pilon's "One feels a golden warmth glowing like a hot enchilada in one's stomach," Danny's "I have here two great steaks from God's own pig," and the narrator's "Big Joe abhorred the whole principle of shoveling. The line of the moving shovel was unattractive. The end to be gained, that of taking dirt from one place and putting it in another, was, to one who held the larger vision, silly and gainless." Surely not only Mordred, but also Launcelot, had no more love for a shovel.

5

ஃ TORGAS VALLEY
AND LONG VALLEY

STEINBECK'S years of struggle to make his way as a novelist—
from the publication of *Cup of Gold* in 1929 to the success of
Tortilla Flat in 1935—were coterminous with the first six years of
the Great Depression. In his own person and fortunes he felt the
misery of the times; yet his first four novels, though they do not ignore politics and economics, betray no deep concern with contemporary issues. Only in *Tortilla Flat* do we become dimly aware of a
surrounding commercial culture whose values have their effect upon
the paisano community. Ignoring the overtones of *Tortilla Flat*, many
had typed Steinbeck as a teller of charming inconsequential tales
about an exotic people. Then just eight months later, in 1936, this
same storyteller presented a novel about a strike, *In Dubious Battle*,
and made his readers face the contemporary realities that many preferred to ignore. Here was no charm or quaintness; here were miseries
and struggles almost unrelieved by a humorous touch. Steinbeck now
began to be typed as a proletarian novelist, but that label was not
accurate either. The gap between the two novels was more apparent
than real; they differ in emphasis, mood, and manner, but both deal
with depressed, propertyless, constantly impoverished segments of
American society. The fruit tramps wanted work and the paisanos
avoided work, but the workers fared no better than the idlers.

IN DUBIOUS BATTLE
Those readers who wanted escape in fiction from sordid reality did
not like *In Dubious Battle*. Others recognized a masterpiece of realis-

tic and naturalistic fiction: realistic in its completely objective narrative and accurately reported dialogue, and naturalistic in its content. For some readers this is Steinbeck's finest achievement—they are not bothered by the objective distance that Steinbeck maintains. In no other novel has he so completely avoided subjective statement: in this book we learn everything from actions and conversations. We stay with a single character, Jim Nolan, throughout, but we see events, not through his eyes, but through our own; we see Jim asleep and, at the end, dead, but we never leave him.

Jim Nolan, unemployed and embittered, joined the Party and went out with Mac, an experienced Party worker, to organize the migratory crop harvesters in the Torgas Valley orchards. They had little trouble in starting a strike, since working conditions were bad enough, but once the strike began they worked hard at guiding it along the Party line. In fact, without Mac, the strikers would have gone to pieces at once, because only he knew how to organize them, how to get them a campsite and food, how to call in helpers like Doc Burton (who supervised sanitation and health in the camp), and how to canvass sympathizers in town. However, the growers controlled the county and had every device of law and means of violence at their command. The strike was doomed to defeat, since the strikers had no weapons or money, and were barely able to feed themselves. Anderson, a grower who had let them camp on his land, ordered them off after vigilantes burned his barn. Mac and Jim wanted the strikers to resist eviction, but had to raise their spirits and give them the will to do so: the men needed the excitement of violence and bloodshed. These stimuli were provided when Jim, decoyed into an orchard, was shot to death. Mac carried his body to the camp platform and began to speak: Here the story ends, or rather, breaks off.

Jim is the central figure, upon whose development as Party worker our attention is focused. Most of the time Mac is beside him and is equally important. Together they represent the Party, which is the real protagonist. Each has a double nature: a true self and a Party persona, and the relation in each between the two natures provides the internal drama of the story as opposed to the external drama of clashing social forces. Jim, defeated and miserable at the outset, finds happiness in Party work, but the Party character begins to take over: he loses his humane and friendly self as he becomes a tough, dedicated Party man, more hard-boiled than Mac, his teacher. Mac, on the contrary, is a thoroughly dedicated Party worker, when we first meet him: he judges every person, object, and event in terms of

John Steinbeck

Party advantage, advising Jim not to like people and discouraging his interest in stars and insects. He has deliberately suppressed his true self to shape himself in the Party image. Gradually, however, his true self shows through: he gives way to passions, as no Party worker should do, and his affection for Jim becomes more and more evident. Near the end he grants Jim's superiority as a Party man and for that reason, he says, he wants to save him. Yet the change in Jim frightens him too: "I've seen men like you before," he said, "I'm scared of 'em." However, in neither man does the second self completely obliterate the first self. Just before his death Jim talked affectionately with Lisa (daughter-in-law of London, a workers' leader); and Mac, still the Party man, could use Jim's dead body as a means of exciting the strikers.

The Party is the protagonist, as Satan is the protagonist of *Paradise Lost*. This organization is called simply "the Party" throughout. Only in an argument between Mac and Doc Burton do the words "communist" and "communism" appear, rather unspecifically. The Party, a collective organism, brings to birth another organism, the union of striking workers. The Party's role as midwife is symbolized by Mac's delivery of Lisa's child on his first night in Torgas, an act that won him influence among the workers; at that time the group organism was born as unorganized and lonely men worked together for the safe delivery of Lisa's child. Two days later the pickers in the Martin orchard were organized around London, a natural leader of men, who now became literally the head of the new organism. The next day this group merged with the groups from the Hunter and Gillray orchards in a well organized camp on the Anderson place. There it thrived and declined, suffering all the vicissitudes of an individual organism. The external conflict occurs between the united pickers' group and the Growers' Association, headed by Gillray, Hunter, and Martin, a powerful and ruthless organism, full-grown and mighty when the story begins. "This valley is organized like Italy," Mac says more than once, and the valley's name, *Torgas*, which means yokes put on hogs' necks, is symbolic of oppression.

From a speech of old Dan, one-time lumberjack, we perceive that this group of workers is itself a unit of a much larger collective person, the entire working class. Speaking of the workers' anger, he says:

"Only it ain't just in one man. It's like the whole bunch, millions and millions was one man, and he's been beat and starved, and he's gettin' that sick feelin' in his guts. The stiffs don't know what's happenin', but when the big guy gets mad, they'll all be there; . . ."

44

The striking apple-pickers represent the whole working class. Correspondingly the Growers' Association represents the whole employers' class, "invested capital," as Mac puts it.

In this novel the collective persons are fully as important as the individual persons. Steinbeck's theory of group organism, discernible in his work from the first, is now seriously employed as a central structural feature of the novel. It is mainly expressed through Doc Burton, and occasionally through Mac, Jim, and other characters. Burton said,

> "I want to watch these group-men, for they seem to me to be a new individual, not at all like single men. A man in a group isn't himself at all, he's a cell in an organism that isn't like him any more than the cells in your body are like you. I want to watch the group, and see what it's like."

Reminiscent of the passage in *To a God Unknown* about the dancing crowd is the description of the excited strikers going off to break through the sheriff's barricade: "The crowd was changing rapidly. The eyes of the men and women were entranced. The bodies weaved slowly, in unison. No more lone cries came from lone men. They moved together, looked alike. The roar was one voice, coming from many throats." Jim told Mac that "it was just one big—animal, going down the road." Mac agreed: "It *is* a big animal. It's different from the men in it. And it's stronger than all the men put together. It doesn't want the same things men want—it's like Doc said— . . . It's a different kind of animal. It's as different from men as dogs are." Doc Burton had expressed the main outlines of the theory: the group animal has purposes different from those of its individual members; they think that they want "the Holy Land, or Democracy, or Communism. Maybe the group simply wants to move, to fight, and uses these words simply to reassure the brains of individual men."

The group animal has its own pathology: the strike, for example, is an infection of the group organism, corresponding to swellings and fevers in individual organisms. Social injustice corresponds to physiological injustice (tetanus, for example) in a man, according to Burton. Revolution and communism, as proposed social therapy, correspond to disinfection and prophylaxis for the individual's diseases. A person in the group may be a special organ of the group animal: Mac might be "an eye cell, drawing . . . [his] force from group-man, and at the same time directing him, like an eye."

The two group organisms, feeble workers and mighty employers,

45

are locked together "in dubious battle." The workers have one friend
—if friend it be—the Party. The Party's uncertain role leads us
directly to the mythical structure of *In Dubious Battle*. Strangely,
although Steinbeck gave the book this title and quoted *Paradise Lost*
(1:101–109) for epigraph, the myth of Satan's rebellion has been almost ignored in critical study of it. But it is not like Steinbeck to
point so plainly to a mythical prototype and then ignore the myth.
Satan's rebellion has everything to do with *In Dubious Battle*. We
must not look for exact correspondences or suppose that every detail
of the novel has a counterpart in Milton's epic or in Revelation. We
need not suppose that Steinbeck must adhere to the mythical sequence of events. There is just enough of the myth present, as in *Tortilla Flat,* to indicate that a strike of humble fruit tramps has universal meaning.

As title and epigraph indicate, it was mainly Milton's version of
Satan's rebellion that Steinbeck had in mind, although Revelation and
Anatole France's *The Revolt of the Angels* contributed, too. Notice
the first words of *In Dubious Battle:*

> At last it was evening. The lights in the street outside came on, and
> the Neon restaurant sign on the corner jerked on and off, exploding
> its hard red light in the air. Into Jim Nolan's room the sign threw a
> soft red light. For two hours Jim had been sitting in a small, hard
> rocking-chair, his feet up on the white bedspread. Now that it was
> quite dark, he brought his feet down to the floor and slapped the sleep-
> ing legs.

Jim had reached the lowest point of his personal fortunes; he was
just out of jail, had no job, and his parents were dead. It is a realistic
picture, and the red light of the Neon sign is part of it. Yet the detail is significant: a red Neon sign's light is not so necessary to the
description of a dismal lodging-house room as are a worn carpet and
washstand. This will be a novel about Reds, but the red light means
much more than that. For *Paradise Lost* opens with Satan lying in
defeat, "rowling in the fiery Gulfe" (*PL* 1:52); there in a "dismal
Situation waste and wilde" he was surrounded by flames: "yet from
those flames / No light, but rather darkness visible," in regions where
"hope never comes / That comes to all" (*PL* 1:60–67). Images of
fire and of contrasting darkness pervade both *Paradise Lost* and *In
Dubious Battle*. Red light and redness in general are more prominent in the novel, but are by no means absent from the epic: for example, heaven's artillery was "Wing'd with red Lightning" (*PL*
1:175), and a "ruddy flame" burns in Hell (*PL* 2:889).

Unwilling to submit to hopelessness, Jim rose from his chair and went to join the Party; and with "courage never to submit or yield" (*PL* 1:108) Satan rose from his fiery couch to gather his forces and carry on rebellion. As Jim slept in the freight car in which he and Mac went to Torgas, "His sleep was a shouting, echoing black cave, and it extended into eternity"; later, dropping back to sleep, "he was in the black, roaring cave again, and the sound made dreams of water pouring over him. Vaguely he could see debris . . . in the water. And the water bore him down and down into the dark place below dreaming." The dream foreshadows Jim's death; but the particulars appear to be suggested by *Paradise Lost.* Satan, leaving Hell's mouth, crossed "the hoarie deep, a dark / Illimitable Ocean without bound, / Without dimension, . . ." (*PL* 2:891–893). He came upon "A vast vacuitie: . . . plumb down he drops / Ten thousand fadom deep, . . ." (*PL* 2:932–934). Recovering, he went on "Ore bog or steep,"

> And swims or sinks, or wades, or creeps, or flyes:
> At length a universal hubbub wilde
> Of stunning sounds and voices all confus'd
> Born through the hollow dark assaults his eare
> With loudest vehemence: . . . (*PL* 2:948, 950–954)

Satan and Jim (with Mac) had the same purpose on reaching their destinations: to persuade subordinate men to disobey their superiors. When trouble broke out in the Martin orchards, the pickers assembled for a strike meeting. Mac told London, the chairman, how to conduct the meeting and what to say in order to have the men vote as he desired. So in the first meeting at Pandaemonium, Beelzebub addressed the assembled demons, urging continued rebellion, and his words were "first devis'd / By *Satan,* and in part propos'd" (*PL* 2:379–380).

The struggle, once begun, is as hopeless for the strikers as for the rebel angels. The angels oppose Omnipotence, who controls the whole world, and who knows all their plans at once. The strikers face the powers that be, the men who control the land, who have mighty weapons and many helpers, and whose spies penetrate the strikers' camp, so that they know their feeble opponents' plans within minutes. They issue warnings and threats, and they make terrible reprisals, in the manner of the Almighty. The analogies of conflict which I have just stated in general terms can be illustrated with remarkable similarities of detail, too numerous to list here. For example, Michael, at the beginning of the original rebellion, blamed Satan for introducing evil into the world and corrupting many angels, and told him that he and his hosts were banished from heaven "to the place of evil, Hell," since heaven must be free of violence and war (*PL* 6:262– 280). Likewise the employers' emissaries, Martin's superintendent and Bolter, blamed the Reds for bringing strife into a peaceful and orderly valley. The superintendent ordered the strikers out of the orchards; if they didn't get back to work at once: "Then we kick you off this place in half an hour. Then we blacklist the whole damn bunch of you. You can't go any place; you can't get a job any place. . . . We'll see you can't get a job this side of hell." And later, "You'll get out of the Torgas Valley. We'll run you out." Finally the sheriff, with threats of Mills bombs, ordered the strikers off Anderson's property and out of the county. Satan called Michael's speech "wind / Of airie threats" (*PL* 6:282 f.), which is epic language for "a sock full of crap," as Mac described Bolter's talk.

Satan's role is obviously played by the Party as a collective person, although Jim or Mac or another may represent the Party in its Satanic role. In contemporary folklore the Devil's color is red. The Party secretary who received Jim's application for Party membership is Harry Nilson—the Old Harry is a popular name for the Devil. Probably the detail of Mac's exhaling steam from his mouth as he ate hot stew is meant to illustrate the identity of the Party and Satan. Particular identifications suggest themselves: London is Beelzebub as Satan's right-hand man; Dakin, attached to his fine truck and equipment, is Mammon; Dick, the "bedroom radical," who employed social graces and masculine charm for the cause, is Belial; Sam, direct actionist, is Moloch calling for open war; and Burke, dissenter and stool pigeon in the strikers' camp, is Abdiel. The strikers' camp, especially at night when lanterns and fires gleam amidst the darkness, recalls the demons' abode in Hell; and the unoccupied and restless strikers, whiling away the time in various amusements or small tasks, recall the demons who, in Satan's absence on earth, "entertain / The irksome hours" in games and wanderings, "as inclination or sad choice / Leads him [each] perplext" (*PL* 2:522–576). And the camp has a humble Pandaemonium in the crude wooden platform from which the strike leaders addressed the strikers' assemblies.

On this platform Mac stood as the story ends. Beside him was Jim's body, leaned against a corner post.

He stood up and faced the crowd. His hands gripped the rail. His eyes were wide and white. In front he could see the massed men, eyes shining in the lamplight. Behind the front row, the men were lumped and dark. Mac shivered. He moved his jaws to speak, and seemed to break the frozen jaws loose. His voice was high and monotonous.

And he began the harangue that would stir the crowd to go on with the fight. So Satan, in his first speech at Pandaemonium, in a moment of defeat, urged his host to continue rebellion. He too stood above the crowd, looking over the massed "fellows of his crime" (Mac addressed his audience as "comrades"); and care, courage, and pride marked his countenance:

> He now prepar'd
> To speak; whereat their doubl'd Ranks they bend
> From Wing to Wing, and half enclose him round
> With all his Peers: attention held them mute.
> Thrice he assay'd, and thrice in spite of scorn,
> Tears such as Angels weep, burst forth: at last
> Words interwove with sighs found out their way. (*PL* 1:615–621)

This final scene of *In Dubious Battle* appears to reflect a scene in the first book of *Paradise Lost,* and Steinbeck appears to end just about where Milton begins. We must notice that the conflict between growers and strikers corresponds to Satan's war in heaven, a precedent event (the subject of Raphael's narrative told to Adam in Books 5–6), but that the beginning of Steinbeck's novel, as I have pointed out, suggests the beginning of Milton's epic narrative, when Satan already lies defeated. Steinbeck draws upon incidents that precede or follow Satan's defeat, as suits his purpose; and so the war in heaven, to which Satan tempted one third of the angels, is run together with the story of the rebels' continued defiance, expressed chiefly in Satan's temptation of man.

To his confederate angels Satan offered freedom, equality, and power; to man he offered the knowledge which the Lord had denied him. The Party is tempter of the workers, offering them a vision of social justice, cooperative democracy, and economic abundance. Mac said to London, "When we get a whole slough of men working together, . . . maybe Torgas Valley, most of it, won't be owned by three men." And through the strike the Party gave them knowledge of social and economic reality: the workers, said Mac, had believed in "the partnership of capital and labor," but the strike taught them

49

John Steinbeck

"how much capital thinks of 'em, and how quick capital would poison 'em like a bunch of ants. . . . we showed 'em two things— what they are, an' what they've got to do."

It is significant that the strike takes place in apple orchards, for any other crop would have served as well. True enough, Genesis speaks only of "the fruit of the tree"; but for Milton, as for every-one, the fruit was an apple; and Eden, like the Torgas Valley, had lovely orchards. In Steinbeck's novel the apple symbolizes the worker's product which he himself cannot possess and enjoy: when men learn to work together, said Mac, "Maybe a guy can get an apple for himself without going to jail for it, see?" Finally the sheriff, representing sovereign authority, ordered the workers out of the orchards. With the Eden parallel in mind we may see significance in Lisa's feeling of shame because Mac and Jim saw her naked when Mac delivered her baby; she referred to that shame in later talks with Jim.

In *In Dubious Battle,* as in *Tortilla Flat,* the principal characters are superficially very different from their mythical prototypes. In con-trast to the gold, silver, precious stones, rich apparel, of Satan's army, the striking workers have battered cars, worn working clothes, and very little cash or food. Their humble platform of old boards simply served the same purpose as the glorious Pandaemonium of the demons. The mythical parallel brings out the universal meaning of the strike: the struggle is part of a conflict which (as Steinbeck saw it in the thirties) has for the twentieth century all the significance of war between angelic hosts in the heavenly sphere.

The theme of war in heaven is interwoven with that of the sacri-ficed god-king. Jim as Party member is Satanic; as a person he is a Steinbeckian Christ. The story begins with his rebirth. When he went to Harry Nilson's office to apply for Party membership, Harry re-marked that Jim acted half asleep, and Jim replied, "I feel dead." Once he had committed himself to Party work he began to come alive: "You're waking up, Jim. You're looking better," Harry said. As a Party worker with a mission Jim felt that he was really living and several times mentioned his new-found joy. Doc Burton said, "Pure religious ecstasy. . . . Partakers of the blood of the Lamb," a sug-gestion which Jim repudiated indignantly: "Religion, hell! . . . This is men, not God." "Well, can't a group of men be God, Jim?" Burton asked. The group organism is divine: it is like Hobbes's Leviathan, "that mortal god"; thus biology merges with myth: the collective organism is itself a mythical construction.

Doc Burton's jest is also an author's hint. Blood is the most conspicuous thematic symbol in the book. Jim's father was a slaughterhouse worker and drank warm blood to keep up his strength. When cops beat him, he went home covered with blood. Finally "he caught a charge of buckshot in the chest from a riot gun," as Jim finally caught a charge of buckshot in his face. Mac insisted on the need of blood for raising the men's spirits and exciting them to action: "A smell of blood seems to steam 'em up"; "What they need is blood, . . . A mob's got to kill something"; "They need blood. That works." This is both a truth of mob psychology and a doctrine of sympathetic magic. As Roy Nolan drank the blood of slaughtered cattle to draw their strength into himself, so the collective person draws his strength from the blood of victims.

As in *To a God Unknown,* a series of substitute sacrifices culminates in the supreme sacrifice of the priest-king himself. First Joy was killed; and immediately after his body reached camp (when London's shirt was stained with Joy's blood), the camp resounded with the scream of a slaughtered pig. Joy as substitute victim had proper burial rites, and his funeral was followed by the slaughter of two cows and a calf, at which Jim was presiding priest, having learned the art from his father: he showed Mac where to hit the animal's head with a hammer and pointed out the neck artery to the slaughterer, whose sleeve was red with blood after he cut the victims' throats. Twice Mac lamented the loss of the blood that poured upon the ground, since it would be good for the men to drink.

When Doc Burton said that he felt sorry for Anderson, who, for letting the strikers use his land, had incurred his neighbors' hatred and risked damage to himself and his property, Mac stated the sacrificial theme explicitly: "He happens to be the one that's sacrificed for the men. Somebody has to break if the whole bunch is going to get out of the slaughter-house." Soon after, Anderson lost his barn, apple crop, and dogs in fire. Later, London knocked Burke out with a blow that tore Burke's jaw and blood flowed from Burke's mouth. A subordinate chief and pretender to leadership (mock king), Burke was the victim needed for stirring the men to break through the road barricades. Jim was shot in the shoulder and blood flowed down his back. Then he began to realize his own sacrificial role, telling Burton that he was ready to die: "If I go out now it won't matter. The thing won't stop. I'm just a little part of it." The sacrificial theme clarifies Mac's use of Joy's and Jim's bodies for rousing the men: it was not merely a callous use of friends' bodies for Party purposes, but also

the acceptance of voluntary sacrifices. When the excitement over
Burke's blood had subsided, and Mac had mentioned the need of
more bloodspilling, Jim said, "Mac, if blood's all we need, I could
pull off this bandage and start the hole bleeding." But Jim was not
allowed so easy a sacrifice: soon afterwards his face was blown away,
and Mac carried his bleeding body to the platform and said, "This
guy didn't want nothing for himself."

After all other sacrifices had spent their force, the crowning sacrifice of the divine king had to be made. Not long before this Jim
had seized control of the strike and given orders to London: he was
in effect temporary king, and now he died for his people. As divine
scapegoat Jim resembles Jesus, who also spoke with authority but
was not actual king. The night before Jim's death, as London sat
beside the sleeping Jim, he twice heard two cocks crow. Jim called
for water in his sleep and said, "Tar over everything." Mac found
him kneeling as if in prayer when the shotgun blast blew his face
away. Mac cried out, "Oh, Christ!" and the exclamation seems purposely chosen rather than another for this occasion. Once as Lisa
holding her baby sat beside Jim on a cot, Doc Burton came into the
tent and said, "This looks like the holy family." There Jim has
Joseph's place; yet Lisa's child, whose birth symbolizes the group
organism's birth, also represents Jim's rebirth. And the name of
Lisa's husband is Joey; that is, the husband and wife who have an
infant boy are Joseph and Elizabeth, Jesus' father and the Baptist's
mother, as in *To a God Unknown*.

The Party, we see, corresponds to Satan, who tempted angels and
mankind; a Party member corresponds to Jesus, whose death saved
mankind. Here is the mythical statement of the novel's paradox. The
obvious link between Satan and the slain god is Prometheus, the
crucified rebel deity who was also human. But is the Party truly
Prometheus, one with the oppressed, or Satan, exploiting them for
his own purposes? Is the Establishment—the Growers' Association
and the government which it controls—a just God who must nevertheless allow evil in order to fulfil his purposes, or an unjust and
tyrannical Zeus? Or is Satan really Prometheus, like Anatole France's
Lucifer? And is his opponent a despotic demiurge, a Milton's God as
seen through William Empson's eyes (*Milton's God*, London, 1961)?
Do the rebel angels have a just cause but a bad leader? These questions remain unanswered as the novel ends.

The answer, in the book's own terms, must await knowledge of "the
whole thing." In this novel, Steinbeck for the first time introduces

the philosophy of non-teleology which he had reached as a result of his biological studies and association with Edward Ricketts. Doc Burton is his non-teleological spokesman, who helped the strikers without committing himself to the cause. He wanted to see the whole picture without putting on "the blinders of 'good' and 'bad,' and [limiting his] vision." He would deal with social disorders as with bodily diseases: "I want to see, so I go to the seat of the wound." Once the whole problem is understood, the remedy can be known; without knowledge men work in the dark. So good and evil, right and wrong become irrelevant; still, means affect ends and "you can only build a violent thing with violence." Doc's sympathies incline to the strikers; but he sees them as an ailing group organism: the wrong that they suffer is an infection that has taken hold of group-man, no more and no less unjust than physical disease.

We may suppose that Doc Burton would inquire into social and economic causes as the means of seeing the whole problem. But he does not, since non-teleology rejects cause-thinking. "There aren't any beginnings," Burton said. "Nor any ends." We may still say that socio-economic factors are part of "the whole picture." But Burton sees "group-man" as the field of inquiry: "I want to watch these group-men, for they seem to me to be a new individual, . . ." The individual members of the group think that they want higher wages, economic security, social justice; but the group really wants something else, maybe just to fight and kill, and it behooves us to find out.

It is just this expression of non-teleology in terms of group-man that is most unsatisfactory in the basic philosophy of *In Dubious Battle*. As a literary device, however, the concept of group organism is effective, since it personifies and objectifies the two sides of the class struggle. The mythical paradigms, Satan's revolt and the dying god, with their ambiguous meanings, universalizing an apparently trivial labor dispute, help us to realize the "dubious battle," the ambiguity of motives and purposes on either side, the uncertainty of outcome (this is Steinbeck's meaning of "dubious," granted that it is not Milton's). The dead Jim is faceless: he has become Everyman.

OF MICE AND MEN

When *Of Mice and Men* appeared in February, 1937, one year after *In Dubious Battle*, readers were not surprised to find that it dealt with agricultural labor in California; for the earlier novel had established Steinbeck as a writer interested in contemporary issues. Yet, if upon opening the new novel the reader expected more about strikes and Communist agitators, he was disappointed; for the workers in *Of Mice and Men* have not yet reached social awareness or class consciousness: they accept their lot, spend their small earnings, never question the structure of society. Here is no Growers' Association to exploit migratory pickers; the men work on a large grain-producing farm (always called "ranch"), managed solely by its owner, who hires hands at fifty dollars a month and found. That is, he has workers who stay with him the year round; others prefer to work for a season and then move on; these are migratory of their own choice. The Great Depression is not yet.

To this ranch came George and Lennie, sent by an employment agency. Lennie was huge and powerful, a good worker, but mentally retarded. He went everywhere with George, who had promised Lennie's Aunt Clara, now dead, to look after him. Devoted to George, Lennie would do anything that George asked him to do. He had a passion for furry animals like mice and rabbits, but so great was his strength that when he stroked them, he was bound to kill them. He also liked women's soft hair and pretty dresses; and whatever he liked, he wanted to touch and pet. In Weed, just before the story begins, attracted by a girl's red dress, he had put his hand on the garment. The girl, misunderstanding his intention, began to scream, and her cries frightened Lennie, who held on to the dress (his regular reaction to fright in such circumstances) until George forced him to let go. Then George and Lennie had to run and hide from the angered citizens of Weed. This was but the latest of a series of incidents in which Lennie had innocently caused trouble.

George and Lennie were not migratory from choice—at any rate, they talked about settling down. They shared a dream of independence, of owning a little farm of their own. George, of course, had invented the content of the dream, and Lennie loved to hear him tell about what they would have on the farm, particularly about the rabbits, which Lennie would tend—provided he kept out of trouble. George's recitation of the dream had become a ritual which Lennie wanted repeated many times. But they were never able to save money, and the dream remained a dream until they reached the ranch near Soledad. There Candy, an old handy man, overheard George's recitation and was immediately interested. He learned that George had a real ten-acre place in mind and could buy it for $600. Candy had $300 in savings and would have another fifty at the end of the month; George and Lennie would have a hundred at the end of a month's work—the dream had suddenly become possible, since they could surely make the deal for $450 in cash and pay the rest later. This was on Friday evening, but on Sunday the plan was shattered: Lennie had killed Curley's wife, the boss's daughter-in-law.

Curley's wife was a tawdry, rather stupid young woman, interested only in attracting men: "Jesus, what a tramp," George said on first seeing her. After two weeks of marriage she hated her husband. She became interested in Lennie because he had crushed Curley's hand, when Curley, a scrappy young man, had made the mistake of picking on Lennie, who looked deceptively like a pushover. On Sunday afternoon she found Lennie alone in the barn and easily enticed him into stroking her hair. Once started, he couldn't stop. She became frightened and started to scream. Lennie, frightened in turn, could only hang on to her hair, and giving her a shake to quiet her, broke her neck. Then he ran to the thicket of willows and sycamores by the river where George had told him to hide if he got into trouble. George came soon, and as he sat behind Lennie, entertaining him once more with a recital of the dream, he shot him with a fellow-worker's pistol at the base of the brain.

The final scene between Lennie and George was foreshadowed by an episode in which Candy lost his aged, evil-smelling dog. Carlson, the owner of the pistol, had persuaded the reluctant Candy to let him shoot the ailing dog, saying, as he pointed to a spot at the back of the dog's head, "The way I'd shoot him, he wouldn't feel nothing." The dog was Candy's only friend, the only creature that he could feel much affection for or that felt much for him; but the dog was a nuisance to Candy's bunkhouse mates and had to go. Afterwards, Candy said to George, "I ought to of shot that dog myself, George. I shouldn't ought to of let no stranger shoot my dog." So when Lennie had to be killed (notice that both dog and Lennie had pale eyes), George shot Lennie himself, to save him from Curley's shotgun.

The dog episode illustrates the kind of dramatic device that Steinbeck employs in *Of Mice and Men,* the first of his experiments in the play-novelette form, a cross between novel and drama. Each of the six chapters is confined to one scene and opens with a description of the scene; there follows dialogue with entrance and exit of characters. Every descriptive or narrative remark can be considered a stage direction (of the Shavian kind at any rate). The chapters can easily be converted, as they stand, into acts or scenes; and this is nearly what was done when *Of Mice and Men* was published and produced as a play in November, 1937. The dialogue was altered very little, and the conversion of description and narrative required more change in form than in content. As drama or novel *Of Mice and Men* is economical, tightly knit, carefully constructed. It is very like a tragedy of Sophocles or Ibsen in its dramatic economy: every word is meaningful in relation to the whole; few characters are used; and prophetic speeches, symbolic properties, and foreshadowing episodes point to the inevitable end.

Man's longing for the land, a favorite Steinbeck theme, appearing in some form in nearly every novel, is here expressed in the farmhand's and bindlestiff's desire for a few acres of his own, so that he can be his own boss. George said, "I'd have my own little place, an' I'd be bringin' in my own crops, 'stead of doin' all the work and not getting what comes up outa the ground." And Candy said,

> "Everybody wants a little bit of land, not much. Jus' som'thin' that was his. Som'thin' he could live on and there couldn't nobody throw him off of it. I never had none. I planted crops for damn near ever'-body in this state, but they wasn't my crops, and when I harvested 'em, it wasn't none of my harvest."

Only in such speeches as these does *Of Mice and Men* seem to relate this land hunger to contemporary social issues. But this is hardly the author's intention: he is simply reporting a mode in which the yearning is really expressed by men whose chances of acquiring land are well-nigh hopeless—altogether hopeless, as Crooks, the Negro stable buck, saw it:

> "I seen hunderds of men come by on the road an' on the ranches, with their bindles on their back an' that same damn thing in their heads. Hunderds of them. They come, an' they quit an' go on; an' every damn one of 'em's got a little piece of land in his head. An' never a God damn one of 'em ever gets it. Just like heaven. . . . Nobody never gets to heaven, and nobody gets no land. It's just in their head."

Yet Crooks too had the dream. When he saw that Candy and Lennie had a real proposition, backed by real money, he offered to work for them for nothing, just to share their independence—until Curley's wife made him realize the futility of his wish. And Crooks was right after all, as the story is told: these were but three more men with that "thing in their heads." The land hunger of impoverished farm workers, a dream of independence, usually remains a dream; and when it becomes a real plan, the plan is defeated.

Of Mice and Men was meant to be a non-teleological tale, and the first title that Steinbeck gave it was "Something That Happened."

Something that happens may be accidental, coincidental, atypical, and surely the concluding events and deeds in this novel are neither typical nor commonplace. For George and Lennie, being who they are and where they are, the outcome may be inevitable, and we may see a personal tragedy in the tale. Steinbeck, however, meant the story to be a parable of the human condition, as his final title indicates. It is a good title, because the story itself tells us just what Burns meant when he said, "the best-laid schemes o' mice an' men gang aft agley": one unlucky fieldmouse lost its nest when the field was plowed. But not all fieldmice suffer that fate; Burns did not mean that no man's scheme is ever realized. Steinbeck reads, "All schemes o' mice an' men gang ever agley." Crooks said, "Nobody never gets to heaven, and nobody gets no land," and George said to Candy, "—I think I knowed from the very first. I think I knowed we'd never do her," thus reading destiny—the inevitable failure of his plans—in Lennie's terrible deed. It is the message of *Cup of Gold,* the vanity of human wishes. In a letter to his agents, written soon after completing the manuscript of *Of Mice and Men,* Steinbeck said that Lennie represents "the inarticulate and powerful yearning of all men," and referred to its scene as a microcosm, making it plain that this novel was meant to express the inevitable defeat and futility of all men's plans. But the tragic story of George and Lennie cannot carry the load of cosmic pessimism placed upon it. It tells us only that it is hard for bindlestiffs to buy land, and that even when they get the money they cannot be sure of making the purchase. Nevertheless, migratory workers have acquired land, even in California, and George could have done so. Not Lennie who died, but Candy who lived, had $350, and Candy still wanted to carry out the plan. Objectively considered, the prospects for success were better without Lennie, who would surely have killed every rabbit on the place. But without Lennie the plan had no meaning for George. The sweeping pessimistic thesis is thus imposed upon the story and obscures its true meaning: that our pleasures often oppose and thwart our schemes. Steinbeck came nearer to an adequate statement of thesis when he said in another letter that *Of Mice and Men* was "a study of the dreams and pleasures of everyone in the world."

After shooting Lennie, an act that the others assumed he had done in self-defense, George went off with Slim to get a drink. This means that George had turned to his counter-dream of independence: freedom from Lennie. This dream, as well as the other, George recited in both the opening and closing scenes among the willows by the river:

John Steinbeck

"God a'mighty, if I was alone I could live so easy. I could go get a
job an' work, an' no trouble. No mess at all, and when the end of the
month come I could take my fifty bucks and go into town and get
whatever I want. Why, I could stay in a cat house all night. I could
eat any place I want, hotel or any place, and order any damn thing I
could think of. An' I could do all that every damn month. Get a gallon
of whisky, or set in a pool room and play cards or shoot pool. . . .
An' whatta I got, . . . I got you! You can't keep a job and you lose
me ever' job I get."

It is a recital that Lennie often heard. At the end the contrite Lennie
expected to hear it again and urged George to say it. George started
half-heartedly, but soon turned to the other recital about the land
and the rabbits. And what George longed for in his dream of individual freedom was exactly what he deprecated in his dream of living with Lennie on a small ranch. He recited this dream too at the
beginning and end of the story, and once in the middle; but only the
first time is it given in its complete ritualistic form:

"Guys like us, that work on ranches, are the loneliest guys in the
world. They got no fambly. They don't belong no place. They come to
a ranch an' work up a stake and then they go into town and blow their
stake, and the first thing you know they're poundin' their tail on some
other ranch. They ain't got nothing to look ahead to. . . . With us it
ain't like that. We got a future. We got somebody to talk to that gives
a damn about us. We don't have to sit in no bar room blowin' in our
jack jus' because we got no place else to go."

Then he went on to describe the little place that they would buy
when they "[got] the jack together," where they would *live off the
fatta the lan'*."

So the "dreams and pleasures" of Steinbeck's statement are both
synonymous and contrasting terms. The lonely bindlestiff dreams of
owning land (and although George said that others did not have "a
future," Crooks said that all ranch workers had that dream); yet he
enjoys cards, whisky, women. His pleasures take his little money and
he never begins to realize the dream. For George, who was tied to
Lennie, freedom to enjoy these pleasures was as much a dream as
having a ranch; in fact, any indulgence in them was severely limited,
since Lennie prevented his earning more than a few dollars at a time.
Thus George was split between genuine affection for Lennie, who was
company, someone to control and look after, and a desire to be free
of an inconvenient burden. When he shot Lennie he was not only sav-
ing Lennie from Curley's cruelty, but was also making a choice be-

58

tween dreams: events had forced him to a decision. "I'll work my month an' I'll take my fifty bucks an' I'll stay all night in some lousy cat house. Or I'll set in some poolroom . . . ,"—thus George answered Candy's question "Then—it's all off?" and realized without joy that one dream was dead and another, the dream of lonely independence, had come true.

Of Mice and Men has no recognizable mythical pattern. The central image is the earthly paradise, visible in nearly every Steinbeck novel. This has meant for Americans an agrarian economy of small farms, worked by their owners for their own benefit. It is part of the American dream, finding expression in such nineteenth-century visions as "the garden of the west" and "the garden of the world." It is a vision of Eden, a land of peace, harmony, prosperity; it includes both individual independence and fellowship. And in Steinbeck's world you aren't likely to get there; as Crooks said, "Nobody never gets to heaven."

We should also notice that this novel ignores the group organism, unless we say that Lennie, representing "the inarticulate and powerful yearning of all men," symbolizes it. Like the group Lennie has an elementary mentality, lacks initiative and originality, and can follow but not lead. The association of George and Lennie, leader and follower, is held together by a religion, complete with myth, ritual, and litany. When George makes his formulaic recitation, as quoted above, Lennie responds at the right place with *"But not us! An' why? Because . . . because I got you to look after me, and you got me to look after you, and that's why."* From loneliness, from blowing our money in barrooms and cat houses, from jails, good Lord deliver us— and grant us the blessings of fellowship on the land. It is a religion of cooperation, but, as in other religions, deprecated evils are powerful to keep men from paradise. The individual's desire for carefree enjoyment of pleasures is the serpent in the garden.

THE LONG VALLEY

If *The Pastures of Heaven* may be likened to Sherwood Anderson's *Winesburg, Ohio* as a series of interrelated stories about a single community, so *The Long Valley* may be likened to Anderson's *The Triumph of the Egg* as a series of unconnected stories strung together on a slender unifying thread. Steinbeck's title indicates a topographical unity, the long Salinas Valley, not a single town or village. And yet the title does not quite contain the contents: "Flight" takes place on the coast and in the mountains next to it, "The Snake" in Monterey. Still, they are set in the same county; but "Saint Katy the Virgin" is a burlesqued saint's legend of medieval Ireland, truly a maverick in this collection.

Most of the stories had appeared in magazines from 1933 to 1938. Only two ("Flight" and "The Leader of the People") were published for the first time in *The Long Valley* (1938). The last hundred pages are occupied by *The Red Pony*, published as a separate book in 1937 (the first two parts had appeared in a magazine late in 1933), to which was now added "The Leader of the People," incorporated as a fourth chapter into *The Red Pony* when it was republished in 1945.

The stories of *The Long Valley*, written over a period of several years, represent every phase of Steinbeck's fictional interests down to 1938, and even beyond, since young Dr. Phillips of "The Snake" will plainly become Doc of *Cannery Row*. "Saint Katy the Virgin," written sometime before May, 1932, looks back as far as Steinbeck's satirical sketches which appeared in *The Stanford Spectator*, and has the Cabell-like touch of *Cup of Gold*. Douglas' *South Wind* had its effect too: as a travesty of the medieval saint, Katy outdoes Saint Eulalia, patroness of sailors. "Flight," like *To a God Unknown*, is prose Jeffers, and is set in the Jeffers country. It is a story about paisanos, but strikingly different in mood from *Tortilla Flat:* it is a grim narrative of suffering and death. "The White Quail," "The Harness," "Johnny Bear," and "The Murder" resemble *The Pastures of Heaven* in certain respects. "The Raid" and "The Vigilante" grew out of the material from which Steinbeck produced *In Dubious Battle*. In "The Chrysanthemums" and *The Red Pony* the reader experiences life on California ranches as the ranchers live it; from the hired hands' bunkhouse in *Of Mice and Men* he moves into the ranch family's residence. "Breakfast," a short sketch, reappears as an episode of *The Grapes of Wrath*.

Here are Steinbeck's best short stories. He published very few thereafter: about six fugitive pieces in journals over twenty years, hardly worth collecting, except perhaps "Edith McGillcuddy." If we subtract "The Breakfast" and "Saint Katy" as sketches and *The Red Pony* as a short novel, we have as remainder nine superb tales, each a masterpiece of technique, realism, insight, and prose style—a style that is objective, economical, direct, and at the same time suffused with a poetic, emotional undertone. T. K. Whipple noticed "the middle distance" that Steinbeck's technique effects in these stories; however it affects the reader, this distance is exactly what Steinbeck wanted to achieve, and he has successfully achieved it. Each story is something that happened, something to be perceived and, in a non-teleological way, understood; it excites feeling and sympathy only as means to comprehension, not as preparation for judgment.

Five stories in the book are named for animals or plants: chrysanthemums, quail, snake, bear, and pony. In addition, sweet peas are the principal symbol in "The Harness," Saint Katy is a pig, a horse is Pepé's companion in "Flight," and a wildcat and puma are fellow-denizens of the fugitive's retreat. *The Red Pony* acquaints us not only with several interesting horses, but also with Doubletree Mutt, a delightful dog (and Smasher has his points, too). We notice how intimately Steinbeck understands the transplanting of chrysanthemums, the raising of sweet peas, the habits of quail and pumas and dogs. Having observed the biological slant of *The Long Valley*, Edmund Wilson was the first critic to point out the importance of biology in Steinbeck's fiction. He put it in a misleading way, saying that these stories "are almost entirely about plants and animals." Rather, the animals and plants have a symbolic function, helping us to understand the human characters, who are really central and really human. Other novelists, drawing images from the organic world, usually see animals and plants as the ordinary man does, and seldom have any special knowledge of them; even H. G. Wells and Norman Douglas, who were trained in biology, use animal and plant images pretty much as other novelists do. Steinbeck sees the lower organisms with a biologist's eye.

Wilson also said that Steinbeck's human characters are rudimentary, intentionally conceived as hardly more than animals themselves; and this judgment of Steinbeck's characters has been expressed often since. Yet when we are confronted with Elisa Allen (again an Elizabeth) of "The Chrysanthemums" and Mary Teller of "The White Quail" (whose character is almost the antithesis of rudimentary), the judgment at once begins to look absurd. Elisa Allen has impressed several critics: Joseph Warren Beach says of her, "She is one of the most delicious characters ever transferred from life to the pages of a book." Mary Teller is a superb portrayal of a narcissistic woman.

Since the several stories are not interrelated and vary greatly in content, we are not likely to find a principle of arrangement for the whole series. It seems to me that only the first three—"The Chrysanthemums," "The White Quail," and "Flight"—were intentionally juxtaposed. Both Elisa Allen in "The Chrysanthemums" and Mary Teller in "The White Quail" are devoted to and revealed in their flower gardens. Elisa loved chrysanthemums; she liked their "good bitter smell." She did all her gardening herself, proud of her "planters' hands," wearing a figured print dress, corduroy apron, man's hat, clodhopper shoes, heavy leather gloves. "Her face was eager and mature and handsome; even her work with the scissors was over-eager, over-powerful." Mary Teller had realized the garden of her girlhood dreams, having married the man who would suit the garden and who had the money to buy it for her. She had a neat green lawn, beds of cinerarias around oak trees, a fence of fuchsias that shut her garden off from the wild chaparral-covered hillside, and a little cement pool for birds to drink from. Workmen did the digging and planting. Thereafter Mary did the lighter garden work, wearing "a bright print dress, quite long in the skirt, and sleeveless," "an old-fashioned sun-bonnet," and "good sturdy gloves." She liked to go to the garden in late afternoon in "the really-garden-time" and sit in a folding chair near the pool. "She was so pretty, so cool and perfect"; she was "like a gentian, so quiet."

Elisa liked her husband, Henry, and was pleased with him when he sold several steers at nearly his own price; and she enjoyed going to Salinas with him for dinner and a show. She was childless as yet, but apparently not from dislike of children. Mary Teller tolerated Harry, since his income was necessary to her world, but she was contemptuous of his business (a loan company). She obviously intended to remain childless, since children would surely be bad for the garden, like the dog which she denied Harry, when he wanted so much to have an Irish terrier pup.

Elisa, although contented enough with home and husband and garden, still could feel the attraction of the itinerant tinker's uncertain roving life. His visit and his calculated interest in her chrysanthemums awakened dormant urges within her, so that she felt like breaking away from her secure domesticity and taking to the open road. When she found that the tinker had thrown away the chrysanthemum sprouts which she had given him—that she had only fancied a sympathetic bond between them—she at first had thoughts of violence, and then with a few tears of frustration composed herself. Mary Teller wanted to sit forever in her unchanging garden. She hated the wild hillside on the other side of the fuchsia hedge; "the wind on the heath" was not for her. "That's the enemy . . . That's the world that wants to get in, all rough and tangled and unkempt. But it can't get in because the fuchsias won't let it." "They were so *right,* the fuchsias, so absolutely right." Only the birds could come in to drink at her pool, and she identified herself with the white quail that came one day. When she saw a cat stalking the white quail, the shock caused her nervous prostration, and she demanded that Harry kill the cat. Harry shot the white quail instead and merely told her that the cat would not come back.

In *The Long Valley* the mythical theme of the garden is fused with the central theme of all mythologies, cosmos against chaos; for in ancient cosmogonies the cosmos has been won from chaos as a garden from the wilderness, and chaos still surrounds it. Mary Teller's garden is a Platonic heaven, changeless and eternal, a cosmos inhabited only by the creator, eternally admiring his (her) handiwork. The hillside represents the world, including human society. That is, our cosmos is Mary's chaos. She is really "Mary, Mary, quite contrary," who had a peculiar but orderly garden, and her husband is the Old Harry (the devil) who intrudes in the garden. In "Flight" (the third story), the wilderness changes its meaning and now represents escape from the world into primeval chaos. Mary Teller and Pepé shun the same human world, but in opposite directions: she from choice, he from necessity. Like Mary, Pepé saw a cat stalking quail and flushed the quail to foil the cat's purpose. For Elisa Allen, however, the outside world of human beings is just what she feels an urge to escape to from her domestic security. Chaos and cosmos are one: "When the night is dark—why, the stars are sharp-pointed, and there's quiet. Why, you rise up and up! Every pointed star gets driven into your body. It's like that. Hot and sharp and—lovely."

In "The Snake" Dr. Phillips' laboratory is a zoological garden of Eden, in which a snake fascinates a woman; but here the woman is the intruder, a neurotic female devil. In "The Raid" the Communists do not consider the capitalistic system to be a true cosmos and want to build another. In "The Vigilante" the usually law-abiding citizen has deserted order for the primeval chaos of mob violence, and then rationalizes his action with clichés of law and order. In "The Harness" Peter Randall was freed by his wife's death from his harness, an unnatural cosmos, to do what he liked, to raise sweet peas and drink whisky; but he could not face freedom in a normal cosmos. In "Johnny Bear" Satan destroyed the Hawkins order in Loma; and in "The Murder" Jim Moore found an old-world Slavic order satisfactory for dealing with errant wives and their paramours.

The Red Pony is a study of Jody Tiflin's passage from naive childhood to the threshold of adulthood through knowledge of birth, old age, and death, gained through experience with horses. It is a story of initiation comparable to Faulkner's "The Bear" (in *Go Down, Moses*), in which the boy Ike McCaslin reached manhood and understanding through experience in hunting and his relation to the great bear. Jody's father gave him a red pony ("The Gift"), and Jody looked forward happily to the day when he could ride him; but the pony caught cold and died, and Jody learned that chance events often thwart men's plans, and that death is invincible and final. The vultures that tore the pony's carcass symbolize the pain and violence that are inherent in the world. In that story a pony was cut off untimely; in "The Great Mountains" the aged horse Easter went off with the old paisano, Gitano, to die in the western mountains, and thus Jody learned not only that all life inevitably ends in death, but that even the aged who have lived a useful life have no other resource. Then in "The Promise" Jody's father promised him Nellie's next colt, if Jody would work all summer on the ranch, and thus Jody discovered that hard work is the price of man's goods. Again things went wrong: Nellie had to be killed to deliver the colt, but the colt was saved for Jody. We are meant to perceive with Jody that death and life are inseparably bound together; such is the world order. In "The Leader of the People" Jody's grandfather, having overheard his son-in-law's unkind remarks, learned that his own world, a time long past, when he led a wagon train west from the central plains to California, has no value for the present generation; his constant talk about it merely bored his listeners, except Jody. Grandfather realized then that the stories are "not what I want to tell. I only know how I want people to feel when I tell them." Jody understood his grandfather and felt the old man's hurt: here was a value and an emotion deeply felt, but brutally rejected by a new generation, busy with its own concerns; and there was no help for this hurt.

In all *The Long Valley* only Grandfather, talking to Jody, has anything to say about group-man:

> "It wasn't Indians that were important, nor adventures, nor even getting out here. It was a whole bunch of people made into one big crawling beast. And I was the head. It was westering and westering. Every man wanted something for himself, but the big beast that was all of them wanted only westering. I was the leader, but if I hadn't been there, someone else would have been the head. The thing had to have a head."

Dorothy Hight Vera

JOHN STEINBECK'S BOYHOOD HOME AT 130 CENTRAL AVENUE, SALINAS

This is what the old man wanted his listeners to feel when he told his stories. The wagon train, he said, carried life across the plains and set it down on the coast "the way those ants carry eggs." And only the ocean stopped them. We gather that if the ocean had not, the big beast would have gone on westering forever.

That may be overstatement, but it matters little. *The Red Pony* is a charming and moving little novel. Steinbeck, remembering his own boyhood, understands a boy's feelings and fantasies:

> Now Jody marched seemingly alone, . . . but behind him there was a phantom army with great flags and swords, silent but deadly. . . .
> Suddenly Jody stopped. The gray army halted, bewildered and nervous. Jody went down on his knees. The army stood in long uneasy ranks for a moment, and then, with a soft sigh of sorrow, rose up in a faint gray mist and disappeared.

Since in the late thirties many Americans looked on Steinbeck as *the* socially conscious novelist, it is surprising how seldom the depression and its problems make themselves felt in the stories of *The Long Valley*. Hard times are mentioned in "The White Quail" but are remote from Mary Teller's world. In "Breakfast" a family of migrant workers are "eating good," and we gather that they had not been eating nearly so well two weeks earlier. "The Raid" alone is concerned with contemporary troubles, but even there Steinbeck's interest in the organizers is mainly psychological. Nevertheless, beneath the level of current events, the inner texture of these stories, their mythical themes, and their biological predilections show them to be stations on the road to *The Grapes of Wrath*.

6

ঙ্গ THE GRAPES OF WRATH

S HORTLY after the publication of *In Dubious Battle*, the novel in which he first gave attention to the plight of migrant farm laborers in California, John Steinbeck made a tour of "Hoovervilles," the itinerant workers' camps, in the Salinas and San Joaquin valleys. He picked fruit and cotton beside the field laborers and reported his observations of their living and working conditions to the *San Francisco News* in a series of articles called "The Harvest Gypsies" (October, 1936), later republished in pamphlet form as *"Their Blood Is Strong"* (1938). Some of this material went into the interchapters of *The Grapes of Wrath*. The harvesters of California crops were no longer Mexicans and Orientals; now most of them were Okies and Arkies, families that had been evicted from their farms in Oklahoma, Arkansas, Kansas, Texas, and neighboring states. They had been tenant farmers or sharecroppers, burdened with heavy mortgages, and natural and economic forces had conspired to force them off the lands which they had called home. Dust storms and erosion exhausted the land and completed what economic depression had begun. The banks and the agricultural corporations (creatures of the banks) found it more profitable to foreclose mortgages and terminate tenancies, combine many farms into one plantation, and put it all to cotton. One man with a tractor could work an entire plantation for wages of three dollars a day. So the farmers and their families were evicted—tractored off, their land plowed under and their houses pushed in, if they

John Steinbeck

failed to leave promptly. Many went west to California, having heard or read that men were needed to pick the crops there.

In the fall of 1937, while returning from New York and Pennsylvania, where he had worked on the stage version of *Of Mice and Men*, Steinbeck drove through Oklahoma, joined migrants who were going west, and worked with them in the fields after they reached California. *The Grapes of Wrath* is thus a product of his own experience and direct observation; its realism is genuine. He was dissatisfied with his first attempt to deal with the displaced farmers' experiences in California, "L'Affaire Lettuceberg," completed in 1938, and would not allow its publication. Beginning anew, he produced *The Grapes of Wrath*, which was published in April, 1939.

It is the story of the Joad family's experiences from their eviction in Oklahoma to their first winter in California. There were twelve in the family, including Connie Rivers, Rose of Sharon's husband. Young Tom Joad was paroled from prison, where he had been serving a term for manslaughter, just in time to join them on their westward journey. With the Joads went Jim Casy, once a revivalist preacher. Starting off with little money and few possessions, having had to sell stock, implements, and furniture at outrageously low prices, they traveled in an old Hudson sedan converted into a truck. The trip took several days. Both Grampa and Granma Joad died on the way, and Noah, Tom's retarded older brother, left them at the Colorado River. From the day of their entry into California at Needles they experienced the hostility of California policemen and residents. The second day, camping in a Hooverville near Bakersfield, they saw the misery and hunger of the migrant workers and the arrogance and cruelty of deputy sheriffs. Connie Rivers deserted them, and Jim Casy was arrested for striking an officer. Leaving the Hooverville just before vigilantes came to burn it, the Joads came to a federal government camp for farm workers where they stayed for a month, enjoying the friendliness, cleanliness, and self-government of this institution. But there was no work in that neighborhood at the time, aside from a short-term job that Tom found. When they no longer had money or food, they drove northwards and found work picking peaches on the Hooper ranch, which provided miserable lodgings and an overcharging company store. The Joads were unwitting strikebreakers, and Tom discovered that Casy, after a short time in jail, was now a strike leader. As Tom talked with Casy, vigilantes attacked the strike committee's tent. When a man killed Casy with a club, Tom seized the club and killed the attacker, receiving in turn

68

a severe blow on his face from another vigilante. Keeping Tom under cover because of his swollen face, the Joads left the Hooper ranch and went to the cotton fields. While they worked, Tom remained hidden in the thickets nearby, until his young sister Ruth was heard boasting to other children that her big brother had killed a man and was then in hiding. Fearing discovery, Tom left his family, after telling his mother that he was going to carry on Casy's work for union of the farm laborers to demand justice. After the cotton picking there was no work for three months. The heavy winter rains came and swelled a creek's waters until the squatters' camp was flooded, just when Rose of Sharon bore a stillborn infant. The Joads took refuge in an old barn on higher ground, where they found a starving man whom Rose of Sharon fed from her breast.

There the story ends *in medias res.* Some readers have objected to the closing scene, in which the young mother who lost her child suckles a grown man. The episode not only has folkloristic and literary antecedents, as Professor Celeste Wright has shown, but for Steinbeck it is an oracular image, forecasting in a moment of defeat and despair the final triumph of the people—a contingent forecast, for only if the people nourish and sustain one another will they achieve their ends. More than that, the episode represents the novel's most comprehensive thesis, that all life is one and holy, and that every man, in Casy's words, "jus' got a little piece of a great big soul." The Joads' intense feelings of family loyalty have been transcended; they have expanded to embrace all men. Another image could have symbolized this universality, but, for Steinbeck, perhaps no other could have done it so effectively.

The novel has thirty chapters, fourteen of which carry the Joad story. The other sixteen chapters (called interchapters even though the first chapter is one of them) take little more than one sixth of the book and are either expository essays or sketches of typical situations in the great migration. They present the social, economic, and historical background, telling the story of all the migrants. With two exceptions the general experiences described in an interchapter are illustrated by the Joads' experiences in the following narrative chapter. Some of these interchapters are masterpieces in themselves. Chapter Seven is chiefly the monologue of a dealer in secondhand cars, who talks to customers, helpers, and himself in quick staccato sentences, revealing his coarse and inhuman avarice. Chapter Five— describing the bank, the tractor, and the tractor driver—presents a dramatic instance of the eviction of a family, and we see vividly what must have happened to the Joads; then in Chapter Six as the narrative resumes, we see the completed act and its consequences. The roadside hamburger stand is as finally and definitively done in Chapter Fifteen as is the train ride in Wolfe's *Of Time and the River.*

As Lisca has pointed out, Steinbeck uses a variety of prose styles in these interchapters. In these short sketches he could experiment, endeavoring in each to evoke both a vivid picture of something that happened and a feeling tone. He employs paratactic Biblical language, go-getter talk, conversational narrative in Okie speech, the sound track of documentary films. Some interchapters are literally poetic. As Lisca shows, if we convert the ostensibly prose sentences into an arrangement of phrases, we get irregularly rhythmic verses that recall the Psalms or Whitman or perhaps Sandburg. An example of this metrical prose in folk-dance pattern may be seen in Chapter Twenty-Three, describing Saturday night dances in the government camps, where the sentences fall into the Chicken Reel rhythm:

> Look at that Texas boy, long legs loose,
> taps four times for ever' damn step.
> Never seen a boy swing aroun' like that.
> Look at him swing that Cherokee girl,
>
> red in her cheeks an' her toe points out.
> Look at her pant, look at her heave.
> Think she's tired? Think she's winded?
> Well, she ain't.
>
> Texas boy got his hair in his eyes,
> mouth's wide open, can't get air,
> but he pats four times for ever' darn step,
> an' he'll keep a-going with the Cherokee girl.

The Grapes of Wrath has little plot in the ordinary sense; there is no complex involvement of character with character, no mesh of events. The story of the Joads could be the true story of a real family. But there is character development, as Tom Joad, "jus' puttin' one foot in front a the other" at first, gradually reaches an understanding of Casy's message and takes up Casy's mission. And the Joads as a whole progress from an exclusive concern for family interests to a broader vision of cooperation with all oppressed people. Lisca has pointed out that the plot consists of two downward movements balanced by two upward movements. As the Joad family's fortunes decline, the family morale declines, too: the family loses members and is threatened with dissolution. But as the family grows weaker, the communal unit of united workers, which came to birth in the roadside camps on the westward trek, grows stronger, and this upward movement is accompanied by the growth of Casy and Tom Joad in understanding of the forces at work. We can put the process another way: the family unit, no longer viable, fades into the communal unit, which receives from it the family's strength and values.

Collective persons are important characters in this novel too, since the plot movement must be expressed in group terms. It can be read as a story of conflicts and interactions among several group organisms: the Joad family (representative of all Okie families), the Shawnee Land and Cattle Company (representative of all Oklahoma land companies), the California Farmers' Association (the organization of big California agricultural corporations, controlled by the Bank of the West), and the workers' union, still immature as the story ends. The Joad family is a democratic, cooperative organism; it is a cohesive group, and yet no member loses his individual character in the group. When the Joads act as a family, they act as a unit: "And without any signal the family gathered by the truck, and the congress, the family government, went into session." It met beside the truck, "the active thing, the living principle," for it was now "the new hearth, the living center of the family." The Oklahoma land company is another sort of organism entirely. It is one of the monsters of Chapter Five which "don't breathe air, don't eat side-meat." Such creatures "breathe profits; they eat the interest on money. If they don't get it, they die the way you die without air, without side-meat. It is a sad thing, but it is so." "The bank is something else than men. It happens that every man in a bank hates what the bank does, and yet the bank does it." As Doc Burton said in *In Dubious Battle,* a group's ends may be entirely different from the ends of its individual members. The monster is the sort of organism that absorbs its members, drains them of their individualities, and makes them into organization men. The tractor is the monster visible: "Snub-nosed monsters, raising the dust and sticking their snouts into it, straight down the country, across the country, through fences, through dooryards, in and out of gullies in straight lines." As the bank officer to the bank, so the driver to the tractor:

> The man sitting in the iron seat did not look like a man; gloved, goggled, rubber dust mask over nose and mouth, he was a part of the monster, a robot in the seat. . . . A twitch at the controls could swerve the cat', but the driver's hands could not twitch because the monster that built the tractor, the monster that sent the tractor out, had somehow got into the driver's hands, into his brain and muscle,

had goggled him and muzzled him—goggled his mind, muzzled his speech, goggled his perception, muzzled his protest.

He had no feeling for the land that he plowed and planted. It was nothing to him whether the sown seeds germinated or not. "He ate without relish" a lunch of "sandwiches wrapped in waxed paper, . . . [and] a piece of pie branded like an engine part."

The monster is in fact Leviathan. In discussing *In Dubious Battle* I alluded to the relation of the group organism to Thomas Hobbes's symbol for the state as collective person, "that great LEVIATHAN, or rather, to speak more reverently, . . . that *mortal god,* to which we owe under the *immortal God,* our peace and defence." Steinbeck's monster is as despotic as Hobbes's Leviathan, but hardly as beneficial to man. He is rather the original Leviathan of Isaiah 27 and Psalm 74, enemy of the Lord. When Casy saw what the tractor had done to the Joad farm, he said, "If I was still a preacher I'd say the arm of the Lord had struck. But now I don't know what happened." He soon discovered the true culprit: "Here's me that used to give all my fight against the devil 'cause I figured the devil was the enemy. But they's somepin worse'n the devil got hold a the country, an' it ain't gonna let go till it's chopped loose. Ever see one a them Gila monsters take hold, mister?" If this monster is a mortal god, he is seemingly invulnerable: "Maybe there's nobody to shoot." But we have seen him, a visible god, in the tractor with its "shining disks, cutting the earth with blades—not plowing but surgery . . . And pulled behind the disks, the harrows combing with iron teeth . . ." Thus, as a participant in the action, the group organism, like the individual characters, takes on a mythical role, derived from the Biblical substructure of the novel.

The Joad family fled the Oklahoma Leviathan, only to run into his brother, the California Leviathan—the Farmers' Association and its typical member, the Hooper ranch, a veritable prison with its barbed-wire fences and armed guards—much the same sort of creature, but even meaner. It is the Growers' Association of *In Dubious Battle,* and its image is not the tractor, but the fat-rumped deputy carrying a gun in holster on his hip. In legend and folktale it makes little difference whether the hero faces a dragon or an ogre.

Leviathan made easy prey of the little fishes, the separate family units. But these units became the gametes of a larger organism, a union of all migrant workers. On the road one family met another:

And in the night one family camps in a ditch and another family pulls in and the tents come out. The two men squat on their hams and the women and children listen. Here is the node, you who hate change and fear revolution. Keep these two squatting men apart; . . . Here is the anlage of the thing you fear. This is the zygote. For here "I lost my land" is changed; a cell is split and from its splitting grows the thing you hate—"We lost *our* land." . . . And from this first "we" there grows a still more dangerous thing: "I have a little food" plus "I have none." If from this problem the sum is "We have a little food," the thing is on its way, the movement has direction. Only a little multiplication now, and this land, this tractor are ours.

In just this way the Joads and Wilsons met on the road; the Joads shared their little money and food with the Wilsons, repaired the Wilsons' car, and joined forces with them for the journey westward.

Then several families came together in roadside camps. Perhaps twenty families would camp together at a suitable place. "In the evening a strange thing happened: the twenty families became one family, the children were the children of all. The loss of home became one loss, and the golden time in the West was one dream." A world was created every evening and dissolved every morning, and was then recreated the next evening, complete with government and laws. And the members, being group-men in a new kind of group, were changed accordingly: "They were not farm men any more, but migrant men. . . . That man whose mind had been bound with acres lived with narrow concrete miles." In Archibald MacLeish's words he now had only "the narrow acre of the road."

The democracy, self-government, and fraternity of the roadside camps blossomed more perfectly in the government camps, where men were orderly and harmonious without police. And the government camps, in which a minority of the migrants lived, were the model for the future commune of all workers. When Tom went away, near the end of the book, he said to his mother,

"I been thinkin' how it was in that gov'ment camp, how our folks took care a theirselves, an' if they was a fight they fixed it theirself; an' they wasn't no cops wagglin' their guns, but they was better order than them cops ever give. I been a-wonderin' why we can't do that all over. Throw out the cops that ain't our people. All work together for our own thing—all farm our own lan'."

Shortly after lamenting that the family was breaking up, Ma Joad, soul of the Joad family, attained the larger vision, agreeing with

Mrs. Wainwright that the Joads would help the Wainwrights if they needed help: "Or anybody. Use' ta be the fambly was fust. It ain't so now. It's anybody. Worse off we get, the more we got to do." At the end of the book the new collective organism is still in its infancy. This is the child that has been born, not Rose of Sharon's that was conceived of the selfish Connie Rivers; and her final act symbolizes this truth. It is a ritual act: she who cannot be mother of a family adopts the newly born collective person as represented by one of "the people [who] sat huddled together" in the barns when winter storms came. It is the family unity and strength imparted to the larger unit. In primitive adoption rituals the adopting mother offers her breast to the adopted child.

The conflict of organisms is necessarily an ecological struggle, a disturbance of an ecological cycle. In *Sea of Cortez* Steinbeck describes a potentially perfect ecological cycle. At Cape San Lucas in Lower California the fishermen catch tuna and bring their catch to the cannery; the entrails and other waste are thrown back into the water; small fish come in to eat this refuse and are caught for bait; the bait is used to catch tuna. But the cormorants "are the flies in a perfect ecological ointment"; for they prey on the bait-fish and tend to keep them away from the cannery shore. So the natives hate the cormorants as subversives. Just such a cycle operated in California agriculture, and the migrants, driven from their homes, were absorbed into it. The agricultural corporations and big growers need pickers in great numbers to harvest their manifold crops. In the thirties they advertised everywhere for pickers with the object of bringing in more job-seekers than they needed; with too many men on hand they could lower wages and increase profits. When one crop was picked, the workers had to hurry on to another crop, if they were to make a bare subsistence. They never stayed long enough in one county to qualify for relief, and so the growers were saved higher taxes. When the time for the next harvest approached, the growers advertised again for pickers, sending handbills everywhere to bring workers back in great numbers. But there were flies in this ointment too: labor leaders, radical agitators, socialists, made the pickers dissatisfied with wages and working conditions, organized them in unions, promoted strikes, and were cordially hated by the growers.

Critics, of course, have noticed the biological features of *The Grapes of Wrath,* but without realizing how literally the monster, the family unit, and the workers' commune are meant to be real organisms. In fact, the biological and organismic side of the novel has been slighted, if not ignored. The mythical side, however, has been much more fortunate, in marked contrast to the neglect of mythical themes and structure in earlier novels. The title suggests a Biblical parallel, since Julia Ward Howe's "vintage where the grapes of wrath are stored" obviously alludes to Revelation 14:19, "the great winepress of the wrath of God." Peter Lisca has accurately pointed to the principal mythical model: the exodus of the Hebrews from Egypt to Canaan. He shows that the novel's three well-marked divisions—drought (Chapters 1-10), journey (11-18), and sojourn in California (19-30)—correspond to oppression in Egypt, exodus, and settlement in Canaan: the drought and erosion are the plagues of Egypt; the banks and land companies are Pharaoh and the Egyptian oppressors; California is Canaan, a land flowing with milk and honey; and the Californians, like the Canaanites, are hostile to the immigrants. Lisca also indicates several specific parallels: the symbolism of grapes to indicate either abundance (Numbers 13:23) or wrath and vengeance (Deuteronomy 32:32); the migrants are "the people," and Ma Joad's words, "we're the people—we go on," suggest a chosen people; in the roadside camps the migrants, like the Hebrews, formulated codes of laws to govern themselves; finally, among the willows by a stream John Joad set Rose of Sharon's stillborn child afloat in an apple box, as the infant Moses was placed in a basket among flags in the river.

There are other parallels that Lisca does not mention. The name *Joad*, I am sure, is meant to suggest *Judah*. The Joads had lived in Oklahoma peacefully since the first settlement, as the Hebrews had lived in Egypt since Joseph's time. But "there arose up a new king over Egypt, which knew not Joseph" (Exodus 1:8); and the monster, representing a changed economic order, and quite as hard-hearted as Pharaoh, knew not the Joads and their kin. In Oklahoma the dust filtered into every house and settled on everything, as in one of the Egyptian plagues the dust became lice which settled on man and beast (Exodus 8:17); plants were covered, as the locusts devoured every green thing in Egypt (Exodus 10:15); the dust ruined the corn, as hail ruined the Egyptians' flax and barley (Exodus 9:31); and it made the night as black as the plague of darkness in Egypt (Exodus 10:22 f.). On the eve of departure the Joads slaughtered two pigs, more likely victims in Oklahoma than the lambs sacrificed by the Hebrews on Passover (Exodus 12). But whereas the Hebrews despoiled the Egyptians of jewels before leaving (Exodus 12:35 f.), the Joads and other Okies were despoiled of goods and money by sharp businessmen in the land that they left.

75

On the journey the Joads crossed the Colorado (Red) River (Steinbeck does not mention their crossing the North Fork of the Red River on Highway 66, although he refers several times to the red country of Oklahoma) and the desert. Grampa and Granma Joad, like the elder Israelites, died on the way. Connie Rivers complained about the conditions into which the Joads had led him, and finally deserted them: the Hebrews continually murmured against their leaders on the ground that they were worse off in the desert than in Egypt, and Korah rebelled (Numbers 16). The migrants' fried dough was the unleavened bread of the Israelites, and both peoples longed for meat. The laws of the roadside camp, like the Mosaic law, forbade murder, theft, adultery, rape, and seduction; and they too included rules of sanitation, privacy, and hospitality. In the camps "a man might have a willing girl if he stayed with her, if he fathered her children and protected them," as in Exodus 22:16, "And if a man entice a maid that is not betrothed, and lie with her, he shall surely endow her to be his wife." The migrant lawbreaker was banished from all camps; the Hebrew lawbreaker was either banished or stoned. Steinbeck's repeated "It is unlawful" echoes the "Thou shalt not" of the Decalogue.

On the road west the Joads met men who were going back to Oklahoma from California. These men reported that although California was a lovely and rich country the residents were hostile to the migrant workers, treated them badly, and paid them so poorly that many migrants starved to death in slack periods. In Numbers 13, scouts whom Moses sent ahead into Canaan came back with the report that "surely it floweth with milk and honey"; nevertheless they made "an evil report of the land which they had searched unto the children of Israel, saying, The land . . . is a land that eateth up the inhabitants thereof"; and the natives were giants who looked upon the Hebrews as locusts. Yet the Joads, like Joshua and Caleb, were determined to enter the land. The meanness of California officers at the border, the efforts to turn back indigent migrants, the refusal of cities and towns to let migrant workers enter, except when their labor was needed—in all this we may see the efforts of the Edomites, Moabites, and Amorites to keep the Israelites from entering their countries.

In spite of the Canaanites' hostility the Israelites persisted and took over the promised land. The Book of Joshua ends with victory and conquest. But *The Grapes of Wrath* ends at a low point in the fortunes of the Joads, as if the Exodus story had ended with the

76

Hebrews' defeat at Ai (Joshua 7), when the Canaanites routed an army of 3,000 Israelites and killed a number of them, "wherefore the hearts of the people melted, and became as water. And Joshua rent his clothes, and fell to the earth upon his face . . ." The defeat came upon Israel because Achan had "taken of the accursed thing," that is, from Canaanite spoils which belonged to the Lord he had taken silver, gold, and fine raiment. The migrant Okies met defeat because they had not learned to give up selfish desires for money and possessions: still too many wanted to undercut the pay of fellow-workers and had no feeling of a common cause. But they would accomplish nothing if they did not stand together. The issue is left there, and a happy ending depends on an "if": if the migrants should realize their strength in union. Casy, Tom, and Pa Joad predict a change that is coming, a better time for the people, when they will take matters into their own hands and set them right. And the author foresees doom for the oppressors: "Every little means, every violence, every raid on a Hooverville, every deputy swaggering through a ragged camp put off the day a little and cemented the inevitability of the day." Only future events will tell us how the story ends: it had not ended in 1939.

Perhaps the most striking episodic parallel to Exodus occurs near the end of the novel. When Tom killed the vigilante who struck Casy down and left the region when it looked as if he would be found out, he acted as Moses had done. For "when Moses was grown" he saw an Egyptian beating a Hebrew laborer, and he killed the Egyptian and hid his body in the sand. The next day when he reproved a Hebrew for striking another, the angry offender said, ". . . intendest thou to kill me, as thou killedst the Egyptian?" And Moses, seeing that his deed was known, "fled from the face of Pharaoh, and dwelt in the land of Midian." In the Pentateuch this happened in Egypt before the Exodus; in *The Grapes of Wrath* it happened in California after the migration. It is another Steinbeck myth inversion. The "house of bondage" is in the new land; in the old land the people had lived in patriarchal contentment until they were forced to leave. It was more like Israel's earlier migration from Palestine to Egypt. Just after reaching California, Tom said to Casy, ". . . this ain't no lan' of milk an' honey like the preachers say. They's a mean thing here." So Moses' task of delivering his people from bondage is just beginning, not ending; it is now that he strikes the first blow. The migrants have gained nothing by merely exchanging one land for another; they must still deal with the "mean thing."

Hence a stillborn child is set adrift upon a stream at the end of the story, rather than a living child at the beginning. It was a "blue shriveled little mummy." This time the first-born of the oppressed had died; yet it was a sign to the oppressors. John Joad said, "Go down an' tell 'em. Go down in the street an' rot an' tell 'em that way. That's the way you can talk." What message? It is given in Chapter Twenty-Five: oranges, corn, potatoes, pigs, are destroyed to keep prices up, though millions of people need them. "And children dying of pellagra must die because a profit cannot be taken from an orange."

Tom Joad becomes the new Moses who will lead the oppressed people, succeeding Jim Casy, who had found One Big Soul in the hills, as Moses had found the Lord on Mount Horeb. As a teacher of a social gospel Casy is more like Jesus than like Moses, and nearly as many echoes of the New Testament as of the Old are heard in *The Grapes of Wrath*. Peter Lisca and Martin Shockley have listed several parallels between the Joad story and the gospel story. Jim Casy's initials are JC, and he retired to the wilderness to find spiritual truth ("I been in the hills . . . like Jesus went into the wilderness . . .") and came forth to teach a new doctrine of love and good works. One of the vigilantes who attacked him pointed him out with the words, "That's him. That shiny bastard"; and just before the mortal blow struck him Casy said, "You don' know what you're a-doin'." And Casy sacrificed himself for others when he surrendered himself as the man who had struck a deputy at Hooverville. Two Joads were named Thomas, and one became Casy's disciple, who would carry on his teaching. Tom told his mother, "I'm talkin' like Casy," after saying that he would be present everywhere, though unseen, "If Casy knowed," echoing Jesus' words, "Lo, I am with you always, . . ." Lisca and Shockley have also perceived the Eucharist in Rose of Sharon's final act, when she gave her nourishment (the body and blood) to save the life of a starving man.

The correspondences between the gospel story and Steinbeck's novel go still deeper than these critics have indicated. Thirteen persons started west, Casy and twelve Joads, who, as we have seen, also represent Judea (Judah) whom Jesus came to teach. Not only were two Joads named Thomas, but another was John; Casy's name was James, brother and disciple of Jesus. One of the twelve, Connie Rivers, was not really a Joad; he is Judas, for not only did he desert the Joads selfishly at a critical moment, but just before he did so he told his wife that he would have done better to stay home "an' study 'bout tractors. Three dollars a day they get, an' pick up extra money, too." The tractor driver of Chapter Five got three dollars a day, and the extra money was a couple of dollars for "[caving] the house in a little." Three dollars are thirty pieces of silver—remember Sinclair Lewis' Elmer Gantry, who received thirty dimes after his betrayal of the old teacher of Greek and Hebrew at the seminary. We should notice too the crowing of roosters on the night when Casy was killed—the only passage, I believe, where this is mentioned—and this at a time when the Joads had to deny Tom.

Casy taught as one with authority: "the sperit" was strong in him. His gospel coincided in certain respects with Jesus' doctrine: love for all men, sympathy for the poor and oppressed, realization of the gospel in active ministry, subordination of formal observances to men's real needs and of property to humanity, and toleration of men's weaknesses and sensual desires. When Casy said, "An' I wouldn' pray for a ol' fella that's dead. He's awright," he was saying in Okie speech, "Let the dead bury their dead" (Luke 9:60).

Casy's doctrine, however, went beyond Christ's. He had rejected the Christianity which he once preached, much as Jesus, starting out as John the Baptist's disciple, abandoned and transformed John's teachings. In *The Grapes of Wrath* John Joad, Tom's uncle, represents John the Baptist, who had practiced asceticism and emphasized remission of sins. John Joad, of course, has almost no literal resemblance to John the Baptist; but he did live a lonely, comfortless life in a spiritual desert, and he was guilt-ridden, obsessed with sin. He was a pious man, a Baptist in denomination; and we hear about his baptism "over to Polk's place. Why, he got to plungin' an' jumpin'. Jumped over a feeny bush as big as a piana. Over he'd jump, an' back he'd jump, howlin' like a dog-wolf in moon time." John, trying to atone for his "sins," was good to children, and they "thought he was Jesus Christ Awmighty." He was, however, the forerunner: for one greater than he had come. When Casy gave himself up to the officers to save Tom, then John realized how unworthy he was beside Casy: "He done her so easy. Jus' stepped up there an' says, 'I done her.'"

It is John Joad's Christianity that Casy rejected. After worrying about his sexual backslidings, Casy came to the conclusion that

"Maybe it ain't a sin. Maybe it's just the way folks is. . . . There ain't no sin and there ain't no virtue. There's just stuff people do. It's all part of the same thing. And some of the things folks do is nice, and some ain't nice, but that's as far as any man got a right to say."

His doctrine of sin led to his positive doctrine of love: ". . . 'maybe it's all men an' all women we love; maybe that's the Holy Sperit—the human sperit—the whole shebang. Maybe all men got one big soul ever'body's a part of.'" And so he arrived at the doctrine of the Oversoul. "All that lives is holy," he said, and this meant that he should be with other men: "a wilderness ain't no good, 'cause his little piece of a soul wasn't no good 'less it was with the rest, an' was whole." In a California jail his doctrine took complete shape as a social gospel, and Casy's ministry became the organizing of farm workers into unions.

In colloquial language Casy and Tom express the book's doctrine: that not only is each social unit—family, corporation, union, state—a single organism, but so is mankind as a whole, embracing all the rest. It is, in effect, a transcendental version of the social-organism theory: Comte's religion of humanity with an Emersonian content, as Woodburn Ross has pointed out. The wine of this new gospel is poured into the old bottle of Christian scripture. Through echoes of the evangelists the author wants to make clear that this is the evangel for our times. The passage quoted above, on the two squatting men who are the anlage and zygote of the new communal organism, recalls Matthew 18:20: "For where two or three are gathered together in my name, there am I in the midst of them." The "crime . . . that goes beyond denunciation," "a failure . . . that topples all our success"—want and hunger in the midst of plenty—that is the sin against the Holy Ghost. The large tracts of uncultivated land that landless farmers could work, and the prophecies that the absentee owners, grown soft, will lose those lands to the dispossessed, strong in adversity and in union, recall the parable of the vineyard: the wicked husbandmen will be destroyed and the vineyard let to other husbandmen who will produce as they should (Matthew 21:33–41). Such owners are like the Scribes and Pharisees, who do not go into the kingdom of heaven themselves, and refuse to let anyone else go in (Matthew 23:13); instead they bind heavy burdens on men's shoulders (Matthew 23:4). Finally, the concluding theme, that family interests must be subordinate to the common welfare, that all individual souls are part of one great soul, corresponds to Jesus' rejection of family ties for the kingdom of heaven's sake: "For whosoever shall do the will of my Father which is in heaven, the same is my brother, and sister, and mother" (Matthew 12:50).

Tom, Casy's disciple, is a Christ figure, too. He seems at first just another Okie, a man quick to wrath who had killed another man in a brawl at a dance, often rough of speech, and not always kind to others. But we gradually become aware that he is different from his kinsmen. His mother said to him, "I knowed from the time you was a little fella. . . . Ever'thing you do is more'n you. When they sent you up to prison I knowed it. You're spoke for." In prison he had received a Christmas card from his grandmother, and on it was the verse "Jesus meek and Jesus mild"; thereafter his cell-block mates called him Jesus Meek. The Messianic succession was complete when Tom said farewell to his mother, announcing his intention of taking up Casy's work and trying to induce "our people . . . [to] work together for our own thing," to take over all "the good rich lan' layin' fallow" ("he hath anointed me to preach the gospel to the poor, . . . to set at liberty them that are bruised": Luke 4:18, quoting Isaiah). Though he would vanish from his parents' sight and they would not know where he was, yet, if Casy was right, if a man has no soul of his own, but only a fragment of the one big soul,

> "Then it don' matter. Then I'll be all aroun' in the dark. I'll be ever'where—wherever you look. Wherever they's a fight so hungry people can eat, I'll be there. Wherever they's a cop beatin' up a guy, I'll be there. If Casy knowed, why, I'll be in the way guys yell when they're mad an'—I'll be in the way kids laugh when they're hungry an' they know supper's ready. An' when our folks eat the stuff they raise an' live in the houses they build—why, I'll be there."

It is not only "Lo, I am with you always" but also "where two or three are gathered together . . . there am I in the midst of them," and it is identity with the hungry, thirsty, sick, naked, and imprisoned, as expressed in Matthew 25:35–45. This means also no hate even for the wrongdoers: "The other side is made of men" too, as Doc Burton said in *In Dubious Battle*. When Tom Joad reproved the one-eyed man who reviled his employer, he was in effect saying, "And why beholdest thou the mote that is in thy brother's eye, but considerest not the beam that is in thine own eye?" (Matthew 7:3).

Jesus is a dying god, and the dying god is the year spirit, the rituals of whose cult are entwined in this novel with rituals of migration and colony-founding. The sunset was red "and the earth was bloody in its setting light" on the eve of the Joads' departure for California in summer drought; then the family congress went into session, and just after that two pigs were slaughtered. The slaughter is described in detail, as was the slaughter of cows in *In Dubious Battle*. The migrants were leaving the graves of their ancestors behind them, personified in Muley Graves. He was stubborn, as his nickname indicates, and he refused to leave the country, although he had no house to live in: ". . . There ain't nobody can run a guy name of Graves outa this country," he said, and "I'm jus' wanderin' aroun' like a damn ol' graveyard ghos'." "Like a ol' graveyard ghos' goin' to neighbors' houses in the night." Then Grampa died before the Joads were out of Oklahoma, and he was buried in his own country's soil. Granma died in the night that followed their arrival in California. The new venture is not for the ancestors; but the pauper's grave that Granma received in California links the old country to the new and the Joad family to another land: this is now their home. Finally, Casy made the supreme sacrifice at a moment when the Joads were down and out. It was already fall; the nights were now chilly (the Hooper ranch must have had a very late peach crop). The Joads moved to the cotton fields and settled in the camp where the winter rains overtook them. The storms were destructive and yet harbingers of the new year: "Tiny points of grass came through the earth, and in a few days the hills were pale green with the beginning year." The migration and the year are one thing.

In no Steinbeck novel do the biological and mythical strands fit so neatly together as in *The Grapes of Wrath*. The Oklahoma land company is at once monster, Leviathan, and Pharaoh oppressing the tenant farmers, who are equally monster's prey and Israelites. The California land companies are Canaanites, Pharisees, Roman government, and the dominant organism of an ecological community. The family organisms are forced to join together into a larger collective organism; the Hebrews' migration and sufferings weld them into a united nation; the poor and oppressed receive a Messiah who teaches them unity in the Oversoul. The Joads are equally a family unit, the twelve tribes of Israel, and the twelve disciples. Casy and Tom are both Moses and Jesus as leaders of the people and guiding organs in the new collective organism. Each theme—organismic, ecological, mythical; and each phase of the mythical: Exodus, Messiah, Leviathan, ritual sequence—builds up to a single conclusion: the unity of all mankind.

To liken the Okies to the Israelites—this too may seem incongruous. Yet the parallel is really close. The oppressed laborers in Egypt were as much despised by their masters as the migrant workers in California. Moses was certainly a labor agitator, and Jesus appealed to the poor and lowly and called rude fishermen and taxgatherers to his company. Again the mythical structure imparts a cosmic meaning to the tale. These contemporary events, says Steinbeck, are as portentous for the future as was the Hebrews' migration from Egypt, and for the same reasons.

The myth is accompanied by symbolic images. As the title would lead us to expect, the imagery of grapes, vineyards, and vintage is abundant. As Lisca has pointed out, the grapes mean abundance at first and then bitterness, which turns to wrath as abundant harvests are deliberately destroyed: "In the souls of the people the grapes of wrath are filling and growing heavy, growing heavy for the vintage." The turtle of the early chapters that persistently kept to his southwestward course has been noticed by nearly every reviewer and critic who has discussed *The Grapes of Wrath*. The snakes in this novel have received less attention. After their first view of the fertile California valley from Tehachapi, the Joads went down the road into it, and on the way down they ran over a rattlesnake (Tom was driving), which the wheel broke and left squirming in the road. This is an omen which betokens fulfilment of the behest spoken in the "Battle Hymn of the Republic": "Let the Hero, born of woman, crush the serpent with his heel." The snake represents the agricultural system of California, which the immigrants are destined to crush. Later Al Joad deliberately ran over a gopher snake; when Tom reproved him, Al gaily said, "I hate 'em . . . Hate all kinds." The Okies do not yet know who their friends are.

Steinbeck left the conclusion of his story to events. How did it turn out? On September 1, 1939, fewer than five months after *The Grapes of Wrath* was published, Hitler invaded Poland and began the war which interrupted the course of events that Steinbeck foresaw. In 1940 America began to prepare for war and was in it before the end of 1941. This meant an end of unemployment. The Okies and Arkies came to work in the shipyards of San Francisco and San Pedro bays; they replaced enlisted men in industries and businesses everywhere; and many, of course, were enlisted, too. They found houses to live in, settled down, and remained employed when the war was over. Mexicans and Orientals once more harvested California's crops, and "wetbacks" became a problem. So did *The Grapes of Wrath* never find a conclusion, cut off by the turn of events? Had the owners learned their lesson and improved conditions? Disquieting reports have been coming from the fields: more Americans are now employed in migratory farm labor than a few years ago, pay is low, and conditions are bad. Perhaps the story has not ended yet.

83

7

᭞ SEA OF CORTEZ

S OMETIME in the late thirties Steinbeck became a partner in Pacific Biological Laboratories, an impressive name for Ed Ricketts' inefficiently managed commercial laboratory, which offered to supply institutions with marine and terrestrial animals of all kinds, alive or preserved, "as strange an operation as ever outraged the corporate laws of California," said Steinbeck after the death of Ricketts in 1948. Ordinarily Ricketts earned enough to maintain himself in the free and solitary life that he relished; he had few wants, few responsibilities, and lived comfortably on an income a shade above subsistence level. But after he became heavily in debt to the bank and was paying out so much in interest that he was faced with bankruptcy, Steinbeck took up the bank loans, "lowered the interest to a vanishing point," and in return received stock in the corporation and a mortgage on the establishment.

Thus, in a sense, Steinbeck became an active biologist. As Ricketts' partner he took a genuine interest in the laboratory's work and, when he had time, participated in it, always, like Ricketts, more interested in the work itself and the knowledge acquired than in prospective profits. Late in 1939, the year in which Ricketts and Calvin published *Between Pacific Tides*, Steinbeck and Ricketts explored marine life on the coast north of San Francisco. Immediately thereafter they planned a scientific trip to the Gulf of California in order "to collect and preserve the marine invertebrates of the littoral. . . . to observe the distribution of invertebrates, to see and to record their kinds and numbers, how they lived together, what they ate, and how they reproduced." They engaged a small boat, the "Western Flyer," for a six-week period, got permits from the Mexican government, and sailed from Monterey on March 11, 1940, returning on April 20. They were in the Gulf, collecting on its shores every day, with two or three exceptions, from March 17 to April 12. Working hard and fast, they collected a great number of marine animals and did not confine themselves strictly to invertebrates. Besides Steinbeck and Ricketts the "Western Flyer" carried its owner, Tony Berry, Tex the engineer, and two seamen, Tiny Colletto and Sparky Enea, Monterey fishermen, who were signed on to steer, cook, fish, and do anything else that needed doing—they even helped collect specimens.

Soon after the "Western Flyer" returned to Monterey on April 20, Steinbeck went back to Mexico, going this time to Mexico City and its vicinity, to help produce the movie *The Forgotten Village*, for which he wrote the script, published in 1941. Then from January to August of 1941 he worked on the manuscript of *Sea of Cortez*, which was published in December. Unless one counts the film script *A Medal for Benny* (published in 1946), this is the only book on which Steinbeck had a collaborator. In fact, Steinbeck wrote the first part, the narrative of the trip—published separately in 1951 as *The Log from the Sea of Cortez*—and Ricketts wrote the second part, a phyletic catalogue. But both men had kept journals during the trip, and Steinbeck drew material for the narrative from Ricketts' journal.

From Cape San Lucas, the southern tip of Lower California, the party moved up the west shore of the Gulf of California to Angeles Bay, and then rounding Angel de la Guardia Island crossed the Gulf to Puerto San Carlos and explored the east shore southwards to Agiabampo Estuary. They stopped at twenty-one collecting stations. The *Log* makes pleasant reading: scientific notes, observations on the animals collected, are mingled with travelogue, philosophy, and *obiter dicta* on all sorts of topics. It is written *con gusto;* it is lively, vivid, and entertaining. We enter into the rhythm of the days, the hard work of collecting, preparing, and storing the specimens, the cruising in Gulf waters, the relaxing on deck after work, the conversations and beer-drinking (beer is almost as important to the *Log* as are the marine invertebrates), the meals and sleep, the visits to Mexican towns. Incidents are given humorous turns. Memorable passages are the accounts of the outboard motor called the Hansen Sea-Cow ("not only a living thing but a mean, irritable, contemptible, vengeful, mischievous, hateful living thing"), the *cantina* at San

Lucas, the youth who found the great pearl, the Mexican boys who guided and helped the collecting party. Reminiscent of Norman Douglas' account (*Siren Land*) of a chicken caught for dinner in a village above Sorrento is the tale of catching chickens purchased from a woman in La Paz: on this occasion too the chickens skillfully evaded capture, everybody in town joined in the chase, and the birds, when finally caught, were already about plucked.

Although Steinbeck reveals little about himself and Ricketts, aside from their thoughts, he tells us a good deal about the behavior and idiosyncrasies of the other four men. We get to know Tony, Tex, Tiny, and Sparky very well—especially Tiny and Sparky, Italian-American fishermen and rounders of Monterey, *paesani* rather like Steinbeck's *paisanos,* men of appetites and humor. And Steinbeck, who felt at home among the Latin residents of Monterey, Spanish-Mexican and Italian, was bound to appreciate the people of Mexico, who have successfully blended Latin and native American cultures. In *Sea of Cortez* he tells about several encounters with the natives of Baja California and the opposite coast. Many are illiterate, he says, and they may be often hungry; they have no physicians and dentists to relieve their aches and pains; but they have a genuine humanity that in many more civilized persons has been smothered beneath blankets of artificial wants, absurd values, and false *personae.* The Mexican Indians whom they met were outgoing in a wholesome way, truly interested in their visitors, and always courteous. They confirmed Steinbeck's doctrine, preached now for a decade, that money and possessions poison human relations if they are lifted above human values.

Nearly every chapter can be divided into two parts, narrative of events and reflections upon them. The first chapter, about organizing the expedition, contains a paragraph on man's "atavistic urge toward danger . . . [whose] satisfaction is called adventure." The second chapter leaps at once from boats to man's atavistic attraction to boats, which is so strong that no man can destroy a boat without feeling guilty of murder; and so Steinbeck turns to reflections on murder as a "diagnostic trait" of the human species (we may feel guilty afterwards, but we do have a habit of murdering both men and boats). Chapter 4 tells about leaving Monterey and going out of the bay into the open Pacific; and again atavism comes into the picture: we are treated to a discourse on "sea-memory, or sea-thought, which lives deep in the mind," inherited from the time when all life was in the sea, and harboring such persistent fantasies as the Old Man of the Sea and the sea serpent. In Chapter 10 the run from Cape San Lucas to Pulmo Reef provokes remarks on scientists and their human limitations, and that subject leads to remarks on the time sense, and that to mutations in man. Chapter 14, the longest, begins with collecting on San José Island on Easter Sunday, March 24; a page of narrative is followed by the "Easter sermon" on non-teleological thinking, the philosophical center of the book. So with other chapters.

Obviously *Sea of Cortez* cannot be underestimated as a statement of Steinbeck's point of view, the interpretation of man and society which he expressed in his novels of the thirties and forties. As Lisca has remarked, *Sea of Cortez* stands in the same relation to Steinbeck's fiction as does *Death in the Afternoon* to Hemingway's. In this biological work we see exposed the biological root of his fictional message. His novels had already made plain that his organismic theory of groups owed more to biology than to political theory, in which during the nineteenth century the organismic theory of state or society had considerable vogue. Almost without exception the theorists had the human animal in mind, looking upon state or society as a compound man. This statement is even true of Herbert Spencer, who, being learned in biology, drew arguments and analogies from lower forms of life to support his organismic theory of society. Before Steinbeck, only William McDougall in *The Group Mind* (1920) appears to have extended the conception to every sort of human group—family, mob, corporation, town, as well as state and national society. The young Steinbeck read Spencer and McDougall; but the book which contributed most to his final organismic theory was W. C. Allee's *Animal Aggregations* (1931). Yet we have noticed that Steinbeck's earliest novels show rudiments of the collective animal. Whether Steinbeck found support in Allee's book for his own conclusions or was stimulated by Allee to further study of aggregations, his organismic theory owes more to actual observations—his own and Ricketts' —than to books. In *Sea of Cortez* he points to the kind of organism that he means when he says that a human group is a single organism: it is the colonial animal like the pelagic tunicate:

There are colonies of pelagic tunicates which have taken a shape like the finger of a glove. Each member of the colony is an individual animal, but the colony is another individual animal, not at all like the sum of its individuals. Some of the colonists, girdling the open end, have developed the ability, one against the other, of making a pulsing movement very like muscular action. Others of the colonists collect the food and distribute it, and the outside of the glove is hardened and protected against contact. Here are two animals, and yet the same thing . . . So a man of individualistic reason, if he must ask, "Which is the animal, the colony or the individual?" must abandon his particular kind of reason and say, "Why, it's two animals and they aren't alike any more than the cells of my body are like me. I am much more than the sum of my cells and, for all I know, they are much more than the division of me."

The first sentence of the individualistic reasoner's answer to his own question is very like a statement of Doc Burton's in *In Dubious Battle*. So not the human being, but the tunicate or sea whip or sponge serves as model for the human group organism. Steinbeck was later to say in *The Pearl* that "A town is a thing like a colonial animal."

The precise biologist may point out that human groups hardly fit the class of aggregation in which Allee puts tunicates, since the individual animals of the colony are contiguous. But to Steinbeck, as to Herbert Spencer, contiguity of parts matters little: he sees the same phenomenon in schools of fish, where the individuals are not in mutual contact. In speaking of the schools he extends the conception from organized groups to whole species, to ecological communities, to all life:

> The schools swam, marshaled and patrolled. They turned as a unit and dived as a unit. In their millions they followed a pattern minute as to direction and depth and speed. There must be some fallacy in our thinking of these fish as individuals. Their functions in the school are in some as yet unknown way as controlled as though the school were one unit. We cannot conceive of this intricacy until we are able to think of the school as an animal itself, reacting with all its cells to stimuli which perhaps might not influence one fish at all. And this larger animal, the school, seems to have a nature and drive and ends of its own. It is more than and different from the sum of its units. . . . In the little Bay of San Carlos, where there were many schools of a number of species, . . . [we perceived] a larger unit which was the interrelation of species with their interdependence for food, even though that food be each other. A smoothly working larger animal surviving within itself—larval shrimp to little fish to larger fish to giant fish—one operating mechanism. And perhaps *this* unit of survival may key into the larger animal which is the life of all the sea, and this into the larger of the world.

And so the state or national society as a single animal is but an organ of a larger single animal, the human species, and that in turn is an organ of the single animal which is the biosphere. And that is not all; the whole world is a single organism:

> . . . species are only commas in a sentence, . . . each species is at once the point and the base of a pyramid . . . And then not only the meaning but the feeling about species grows misty. One merges into another, groups melt into ecological groups until the time when what we know as life meets and enters what we think of as non-life: barnacle and rock, rock and earth, earth and tree, tree and rain and air. And the units nestle into the whole and are inseparable from it.

Here is the Oversoul (to which Steinbeck alludes in the "Easter sermon"), and here is the great chain of being. Steinbeck's statement is near to Leibniz':

> Thus men are linked with the animals, these with the plants and these with the fossils, which in turn merge with those bodies which our senses and our imagination represent to us as absolutely inanimate. . . . it is necessary that all the orders of natural beings form but a single chain, in which the various classes, like so many rings, are so closely linked one to another that it is impossible for the senses or the imagination to determine precisely the point at which one ends and the next begins—all the species which, so to say, lie near to or upon the borderlands being equivocal, and endowed with characters which might equally well be assigned to either of the neighboring species. (Lovejoy's translation.)

Steinbeck is certainly Leibnizian when he says that life "is a unified field of reality" in which "everything is an index of everything else." The "feeling we call religious," says Steinbeck, is "the attempt to say that man is related to the whole thing."

In these higher pantheistic and panpsychic reaches we leave biology behind. Although his biological studies of animal aggregations shaped Steinbeck's organismic theory of the human group, biological science does not really support it; that is, all the evidence that he adduces can be, and is, explained otherwise. Steinbeck himself designates all such speculation as "It might be so." Since in *To a God Unknown* he had already stated through Joseph Wayne the central idea expressed in the foregoing quotations, it is probable that his belief in the unity of all being was prior to his formulation of the group-organism theory as a special application of it. It may be that his reading of Emerson and Emerson's Romantic predecessors first turned his mind in this direction. For the organic view of the world is a distinctive and fundamental feature of Romantic thought. The Romantics, re-

volting against mechanistic and formistic ideas, turned to the world
of living things for a cosmic pattern. They likened the world to a
living animal or plant, as Morse Peckham has shown: "[The meta-
phor] is a tree, for example; and a tree is a good example," being
an image that they used often. The interrelation of a tree's component
parts is that "of leaves to stem to trunk to root to earth. Entities are
an organic part of that which produced them. The existence of each
part is made possible only by the existence of every other part."

Steinbeck has much in common with the Romantics. He is usually
classed as a realist or naturalist, but these are mere labels, and they
hardly suit *To a God Unknown* and *Tortilla Flat*. Moreover, Irving
Babbitt the anti-Romantic and Jacques Barzun the pro-Romantic
agree on one thing, that realism springs from Romanticism. But in a
deeper sense than that, Steinbeck is an heir of the Romantic movement. The organic view of the world renews primitive animism at a
more sophisticated level. To the animist, sky and earth, wind and
storm, tree and rock are living entities. Out of animism springs myth,
and so Steinbeck's biological interpretation and his mythical interpretation of the human condition flow from one and the same source.

In his discourse on the schools Steinbeck recurs to the idea expressed in *In Dubious Battle* that an individual may be a special
organ of the group animal:

> . . . we suspect that when the school is studied as an animal . . . ,
> it will be found that certain units are assigned special functions to
> perform; that weaker or slower units may even take their places as
> placating food for the predators for the sake of the security of the
> school as an animal. . . . There would seem to be only one com-
> mandment for living things: Survive! And the forms and species and
> units and groups are armed for survival, fanged for survival, timid
> for it, fierce for it, clever for it, poisonous for it, intelligent for it.
> This commandment decrees the death and destruction of myriads of
> individuals for the survival of the whole.

One function of the individual unit, then, is to die for the good of the
whole. Here and elsewhere Steinbeck asserts that the relation of
predator to prey is mutually beneficial: in Norway, it seems, the
hawks were doing the willow grouse a good turn by preying on them,
killing those slow-moving grouse infected with a parasitic disease and
thus preventing the spread of the disease to healthy birds. This leads
to the conclusion, and Steinbeck does not hesitate to draw it, that no
individual's death matters at all, since it is necessary for the survival

of the species; the commandment "Survive" is directed to the collective beings. For "to the whole, there is no waste. The great organism, Life, takes it all and uses it all. . . . Nothing is wasted; 'no star is lost.'" Even human sacrifice can be rationalized:

> Sometimes one has a feeling of fullness, of warm wholeness, wherein every sight and object and odor and experience seems to key into a gigantic whole. . . . Perhaps among primitive peoples the human sacrifice has the same effect of creating a wholeness of sense and emotion—the good and bad, beautiful, ugly, and cruel all welded into one thing. Perhaps a whole man needs this balance.

Thus natural selection and sacrament have the same meaning, and magic is truly the forerunner of science. The sacrifices of Joseph Wayne, Jim Nolan, and Jim Casy expressed an at-one-ment with the universe.

To the pantheist the world must be exactly as it is, and everything has its place—cruelty, pain, crime, death. To the biological pantheist the universe is one great ecological community: every unit has its niche and is related to every other unit. In such a world blame is out of the question; we cannot even speak of causes, because everything is just what it is, and every fact "[is] so because it's so." This is what Steinbeck means by non-teleological thinking. Was it by design that Steinbeck and Ricketts "discussed intellectual methods and approaches" as they collected on Easter Sunday? At any rate this was one day among others. They rejected what they called teleology, thinking in terms of cause-effect and end patterns, since, they held, this kind of thinking is both superficial and fallacious, prone to the *post hoc, ergo propter hoc* error. The teleologist asks "Why?" and is easily satisfied with an answer that assigns a cause. The non-teleologist asks, not "Why?" but "How?" and "What?" (can he really answer "What?" more easily than "Why?"). He is not satisfied until he has seen the whole picture, which, of course, he never can see completely. Steinbeck calls it "'is' thinking," a tough-minded, statistical, relational way of dealing with phenomena, which brings a deeper understanding and acceptance. The key word here is "acceptance": action for change may be indicated when all conditions of a problem have been discovered, as when a physician correctly prescribes after making a correct diagnosis; but in general one will be satisfied with things as they are, having understood. To take Steinbeck's preliminary example: what does one do about unemployment (as it still stood in America in 1939–40)? Nothing, apparently, since the non-teleological investigator, looking at conditions "as is," would discover that there were jobs for only seventy per cent of the labor force. Today we would say that the non-teleologist was as easily satisfied that he had seen the whole picture as was the teleologist that he had found the cause.

Of course, there is some soundness in Steinbeck's position. The critique of causality has a history two centuries old. And it is true that cause has sometimes meant blame: Greek *aitia* (first element in *aetiology*), for instance, has both meanings. The fact remains that Steinbeck and Ricketts set up a straw man. The "teleological" answers which they give to the model questions (e.g., "Why are some men taller than others?") are superficial, and yet they put these answers on the same level with the cause-effect sequences of physics. They have confused final causes, against which their case is good, with efficient causes, which we cannot eliminate from our thinking (nor did they). Physicists are as well aware as they of statistical methods and continuous processes, but physicists properly apply the term "cause" to that event or operation which must take place before another can. Whether we say "outgrowth" with Steinbeck or "result" with most scientists makes no difference. As for blame-thinking, Isaiah Berlin (in *Historical Inevitability*) has attacked the search for causality in history on the ground that it does not let us blame the malefactors of history.

Nothing would seem more rationalistic and non-religious than this positivistic philosophy, and yet it is purposely placed in the chapter concerned with the events of Easter Sunday. Non-teleology is a new gospel, properly proclaimed upon this day; it is "the 'new thing,' the Hegelian 'Christ-child' " (although Christmas would seem the more appropriate occasion for that). Steinbeck compares it "to the triangle, to the Christian ideas of trinity, to Hegel's dialectic, and to Swedenborg's metaphysic of divine love (feeling) and divine wisdom (thinking)." It amounts to a grand reconciliation: everybody—Jesus, Francis, Darwin, Einstein—has been saying the same thing in different vocabularies.

The ideas expressed in *Sea of Cortez,* although receiving complete articulation and formulation here for the first time, underlie all Steinbeck's novels of the thirties. *To a God Unknown* obviously expresses the same panpsychic view of the world: Joseph Wayne could have made the statement which Steinbeck attributes to an imaginary Gulf Indian: ". . . I am the whole thing, . . . I ought to know when I

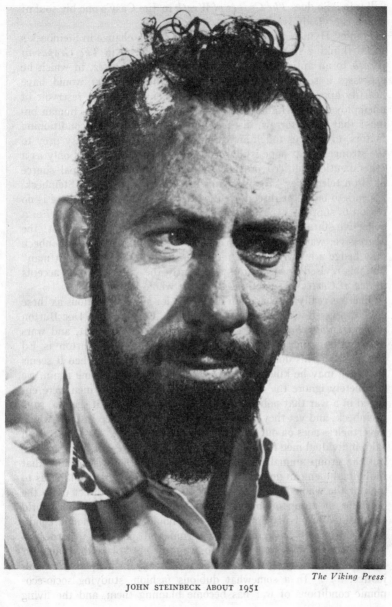

JOHN STEINBECK ABOUT 1951

will rain." So does *The Grapes of Wrath* in Jim Casy's one big soul of which everybody is a part.

Stanley Hyman and other critics have seen a change in Steinbeck's social thinking from a kind of agrarian socialism in *The Grapes of Wrath* to an antisocial individualism in *Sea of Cortez,* in which he expresses a social Darwinism which Herbert Spencer would have heartily approved. He makes such statements as that a reservoir of unemployed is inevitable; that war is a diagnostic trait of human beings; that pain, sorrow, disease, hunger, are necessary conditioning factors, to keep us tough and prevent our becoming an easy prey to the stronger; that hope is illusory, a diagnostic trait useful only as a "therapeutic poultice" or shock-absorber, and the principal source of "iron teleologies." Again, man's present mutation, says Steinbeck, appears to be in the direction of greater collectivism and "there is no reason to suppose . . . [that this mutation] is for the better." For a collective state, like that of the Incas, becomes soft and corrupt: the aggressive, warlike Spaniards destroyed the Inca empire. Steinbeck may hedge a bit with an "It might be so" or a "viewing-point man" but this revised Spencerism is apparently the view which he accepts in *Sea of Cortez* as something like "the whole picture."

There is really no change in his views, for such convictions as these were expressed in his novels of the thirties. For example, Doc Burton of *In Dubious Battle* saw labor troubles, unemployment, and wars as afflictions and drives of the group animal. Doc Burton is Ed Ricketts, and his doctrine dominates *Sea of Cortez:* "When it seems that men may be kinder to men, that wars may not come again, we completely ignore the record of our species." In 1940 men were engaged in a war that nobody wanted (not even Hitler, it seems), says Steinbeck, and yet they had it, "a zombie war of sleep-walkers which nevertheless goes on out of all control of intelligence." As Doc Burton said, individual men formulate reasons and purposes for going to war, but the group animal merely wants war, and there is nothing that individual men can do about it. So these non-teleologists, telling us to look at the whole picture, to see what actually "is," direct us to the behavior of group organisms which are all part of the one world organism. We might suppose that we should study economic conditions, historical backgrounds, governmental policies, in order to arrive at the whole picture. But no, we must not "place the blame for killing and destroying on economic insecurity, on inequality, on injustice, . . ." In a somewhat dubious fashion, studying socio-economic conditions of war has become blaming them, and the living actions, decisions, oppressions, become three abstractions that can be dismissed at once. One begins to suspect that "the whole picture" is preconceived.

Steinbeck's non-teleological speculations are the foundation of his social Darwinism, organismic theory, and chain of being (the last in striking agreement with Leibniz, whose philosophy is thoroughly teleological). These are uneasy bedfellows, since social Darwinism favors aggression, go-getting, business success, heaping up of riches; whereas the organismic and panpsychic ideas look toward cooperation, harmony, and the family virtues—there are reprehensible groups, but, like bad individuals, they are out of tune. Hence Steinbeck finds an ethical paradox, to which he recurs in *Cannery Row:* that though we profess love "of wisdom, tolerance, kindliness, generosity, humility," and hate "of cruelty, greed, self-interest, graspingness, and rapacity," yet the approved "good qualities are invariable concomitants of failure, while the bad ones are the cornerstones of success." Men, he continues, secretly admire the bad qualities which bring success and riches, and though they regard Jesus, Augustine, and Socrates with love, they "would rather be successful than good." So if a biologist objectively observed these phenomena in another species, he "would replace the term 'good' with 'weak survival quotient' and the term 'bad' with 'strong survival quotient.' " Here Steinbeck puts his finger on a conflict of moralities in our civilization, but he has lapsed into the social-Darwinistic equation of survival with success in economic competition (and overlooked the present reality, that competition no longer accurately describes the economy), which means the acquisition of that property and wealth which cut one off from the "we." Nevertheless, all the heroes of his novels for a decade illustrated the good qualities of friendliness, generosity, humility (though not always honesty): his paisanos are healthy when they have nothing to do with the values of property and business success and go into decline as soon as they acquire property. His point had been that these values did not matter and that no real success was won in realizing them. So he appears to express inconsistent views about viable qualities: the ruthless wealth-seeker has a "strong survival quotient," and the poor but honest man has a healthier and more satisfactory way of life. Steinbeck attempts to reconcile these views by pointing to a "routine of changing domination." The successful rich become soft in security and are replaced by men who had become strong in adversity; then the new dominants become soft in their turn. In *The Grapes of Wrath*, Ma Joad told Tom that hardships make the people

95

tough: "Rich fellas come up an' they die, an' their kids ain't no good, an' they die out. But, Tom, we keep a-comin'." And in interchapters of that novel Steinbeck shows that property and too great security have corrupted the owners, making them soft or dehumanizing them, whereas the pickers gain strength in adversity. But the point of the dominance-cycle theory is that success, survival, is gained through the bad qualities which are its concomitants. That is, the unsuccessful good men, toughened by hardships, adopt the bad aggressive qualities and win. The Joads, however, moved in precisely the opposite direction, towards greater friendliness and generosity; for their contingent success lay in the direction of greater cooperation and union with other men. The truth is that Steinbeck (and Ricketts) did not think the question through. With his natural selection in human affairs and his group organism he had stopped with Herbert Spencer, who died in 1903.

Steinbeck's "agrarian socialism" is really Chestertonian Distributivism, a society of small-scale farmers working their own plots. First, the men who want land must be given some; second, the present owners must realize this or go under. In *The Grapes of Wrath* Steinbeck lectures the owners: "If you who own the things people must have could understand this, you might preserve yourself. . . . For the quality of owning freezes you forever into 'I,' and cuts you off forever from the 'we.' " That is, they do not recognize their human and cosmic identity, are no longer in harmony with nature, and are therefore vulnerable. Aroused by the migrants' problems, Steinbeck expressed his characteristic views in social terms and envisaged a cooperative society based on small landholdings. Despite this, the vision was fitful; *In Dubious Battle* and *The Grapes of Wrath* waver between optimism and doubt and end without coming to a conclusion. Shortly afterwards in the Gulf of California, as Steinbeck repeatedly tells us, world and national affairs became remote. A world war was going on, and the collecting party hardly gave it a thought.

With Chesterton I believe that the most important thing about a man is his view of the world, and when we know Steinbeck's philosophy the meaning of his novels becomes clearer. And since it is an inadequate philosophy for a novelist, the central theses of his novels are not likely to carry complete conviction, whatever his narrative and poetic skill. Here is the big fault. Great as Steinbeck's novels of the thirties are, and they are truly great, they fall short of eminence, simply because Steinbeck lacked a genuine theory of society; for the group organism will not do. He was constantly trying to put man in relation to the universe instead of to his fellows, like the Akkadian mythmaker who started from creation in order to define toothache's place in the world. One might almost say that Steinbeck's characters do not have social relations; certainly they do not have them as do the characters of Henry James, Dickens, George Eliot, Stendhal, or Faulkner.

One can learn something about marine zoology from Steinbeck's *Log* as well as from Ricketts' phyletic catalogue. The book is a contribution to zoological science both valuable and useful. A pleasant feature is Steinbeck's evident love of the work that he was doing and admiration for the creatures that he observed and collected.

8

~§ THE MORALITIES

N OW THE great days are done. Since *The Grapes of Wrath* and
Sea of Cortez Steinbeck has written nine novels and four other
books. Each has received varied responses from critics and readers;
each has had its defenders; but in general the nay-sayers have been
more numerous. Steinbeck's admirers have opened each new book
with hope and many of them have experienced in each some measure
of disappointment—unless an appreciator has thought enough of
Cannery Row or *East of Eden* to say that it has approached the
earlier heights. These two books show, at least, that the decline has
not been unbroken, but to what extent they show renewed powers is
a question that each reader will answer differently.

THE MOON IS DOWN

Immediately after completing the manuscript of *Sea of Cortez*,
Steinbeck, now intensely interested in the current war, started work
on *The Moon Is Down*, his second experiment in the play-novelette
form. It was published just seven months later, in March of 1942
(and as a play in 1943). The short span of time from inception to
final publication indicates a hasty job, and the book shows it. Steinbeck wanted to aid the resistance movements in Europe; he later
called this book "a kind of celebration of the durability of democracy." But although we are told in the novel that free men in a
democracy have a strength that tyranny cannot break, the narrative
does not support this thesis.

The scene is a town on the coast of a peaceful country which an aggressive power has taken over. Colonel Lanser, in command of the occupying force, and his staff of four men made their headquarters in the mayor's palace. The colonel wanted to issue ordinances and order executions of civilians through Mayor Orden, whom he kept in office. Orden, however, would not cooperate with the invaders, who in time began to feel the people's hatred for them. Acts of sabotage became so numerous that Lanser, advised by Corell, the local quisling, held Orden's life in pledge for the community's behavior. The story ends with Orden going out to face a firing squad.

Steinbeck did not specify time and place, meaning this to be a parable of democracy against tyranny. The invaders are never called Germans, although Lanser had served in an army that occupied Belgium and northern France in the First World War. The occupied country is never called Norway, although inhabitants have such names as Orden, Anders, Winter; and men cross the sea to England. Hitler and Nazis are never mentioned, although the invaders have a revered Leader. It will be convenient to call the invaders Germans and the townsmen Norwegians.

The officers are patriotic Germans, but do not appear to be dedicated Nazis, and, with one exception, are not militarists. They want Germany to win; they carry out orders; but they are not personally harsh, brutal, or ruthless. They are human, even kind, and take a good deal of insult and even injury rather meekly. Steinbeck was trying to remember that "the other side is made of men" too; but his rather pleasant German officers caused a storm of criticism to fall upon the book from the day of its publication. In the passions of wartime, readers did not like such a dispassionate view of Hitler's agents. Passions have long since subsided, but readers still find something wrong about Steinbeck's Germans.

In his essay, "My Short Novels" (1953), Steinbeck says, "I had written of Germans as men, not supermen, and this was considered a very weak attitude to take," and he thought that events had justified him. The fault, however, does not lie in his attempt to reveal the humanity of German officers, but in the false humanity that he gave them. These men do not ring true; they are like sentimental Americans. Steinbeck may say that he was generalizing, that these men were any totalitarian aggressors and not meant to be really German occupiers—but if so, what relevance did the story have to the contemporary resistance movements? For no German occupation officer acted or thought like Lanser. If this had been a study of a genuine occupation commander, a convinced Nazi, revealing his human traits,

99

good and bad, his inner conflicts and doubts—something that Thomas Mann might have done—it could have been a valuable book. Lanser is skeptical and cynical about his superiors and their principles; he hates war because he has seen it; he does not want to treat the townsmen harshly, but has to carry out his superiors' orders. To paraphrase *The Grapes of Wrath*, "It happens that every man in the German army hates what the German army does, and yet the German army does it. The German army is something more than men." Germany, as Steinbeck sees it, simply wants to make war and oppress people—that is the nature of the beast—whereas the individual German, as something more than the division of the group animal, may have quite decent individual purposes and may attribute noble purposes to Germany. Lanser said to Orden, ". . . what I think . . . is of no importance. I might agree with you, but that would change nothing. The military, the political pattern I work in has certain tendencies and practices which are invariable." Lanser, of course, is a non-teleologist.

The Norwegian town is a Steinbeck community: it is like a colonial animal. News and rumor run quickly through it; it is homogeneous and united; mayor and people think alike; the mayor as head is always aware of the people's feelings, because he feels exactly as they do about everything. Except for Corell, really an outsider, this was a town without factions, thoroughly democratic, founded on a tradition four centuries old. But it is a town that has been too peaceful and secure, and it fell with barely a struggle to the invader. Still, the characteristics which made it secure and vulnerable are those which give it the will to resist and make it invincible. It will undermine the enemy with silent contempt and persistent acts of sabotage; but the narrative hardly convinces us that this is so, particularly when the sage head of the town is executed at the end. There is truth in that incident; but we have to assume, if Steinbeck is right, that Hitler's Germans would never terrorize the population, move it elsewhere, or wipe it out (since they could use captive labor in the coal mines).

There is an underlying myth, the tale of Judith and Holofernes, but it hardly gives the novel its structure. Alex Morden, a miner, killed a German officer, Captain Bentick, and was shot by a firing squad commanded by Lieutenant Tonder. Later Tonder, attracted to Molly, Morden's widow, approached her; she led him to believe that she would accept him if he would bring her two sausages (or any food), but she put scissors inside her dress before meeting him, and with that weapon she killed him. Thus Judith lured Holofernes with a false promise of her favors and killed him after sitting at dinner with him. As Judith said, "O God, O my God, hear me also a widow," before going to Holofernes' tent, so Molly said, "God keep me!" But Molly's deed did not deliver her town, as Judith's delivered Bethulia from the Assyrians.

The final chapter is meant to equate Mayor Orden with Socrates and his executioners with the Athenians who put Socrates to death, for Mayor Orden, just before going forth to die, recited passages from Socrates' *Apology*. The parallel, however, is a bit forced. Like several Steinbeck titles, *The Moon Is Down* is a quotation, taken from *Macbeth*. At the beginning of the first scene in Act II, Banquo on his way to Macbeth's castle, where Duncan lies, asks Fleance, "How goes the night, boy?" and Fleance answers, "The moon is down; I have not heard the clock." Earlier quotation-titles, *In Dubious Battle* and *The Grapes of Wrath*, suggested the mythical or literary precedent, but *The Moon Is Down* resembles *Macbeth* only in one respect: like Macbeth, the Germans, once embarked on a course of murder, are forced to commit more murders. The title, I believe, is intended only to equate Nazi-occupied Europe (or the contemporary state of the world) with darkest night.

As Stanley Hyman has suggested, Steinbeck was trying to adjust his wartime democratic commitment to his philosophy as expressed in *Sea of Cortez* and could not make them congruent. The book has its merits, but it shows plainly the inadequacies of Steinbeck's interpretation of society and history.

CANNERY ROW

World War II was nearing its end when *Cannery Row* (dated 1945) was published at the end of 1944. It makes no reference to the war, for its dramatic date is set in the thirties, and aside from one reference to unemployment the depression is ignored, too. It was, however, meant to provide more than a relief from war: beneath its humor lurks a criticism of American culture. Steinbeck agreed with Malcolm Cowley that the book was a "poisoned cream puff."

Superficially the book resembles *Tortilla Flat*. The story is built around a group of bums on Cannery Row, a stretch of Monterey waterfront occupied by fish canneries. They are American bums, not paisanos. Mack dominates a company—Hughie, Eddie, Jones, Gay, Hazel—who occupy an old storage shed which they call the Palace Flophouse and Grill. They share the center of the stage with Doc, owner and operator of Western Biological Laboratory, a one-man enterprise like Ed Ricketts' Pacific Biological Laboratories, and situated like it on Cannery Row. Mack and his friends, wanting to do something nice for Doc, planned a surprise party for him. They gave it in his laboratory on an evening when they expected his return from a collecting trip; but he did not get back until the party was over and had ended in a brawl that wrecked his place. Finally the boys organized a successful party for the evening of what they supposed to be Doc's birthday.

The narrative course is interrupted by interchapters which are not so systematically inserted as are those of *The Grapes of Wrath,* nor is their relation to contiguous narrative chapters so easy to comprehend. All but two are flashbacks or digressions which inform us about persons and places that appear in the story, much like certain chapters in Norman Douglas' *South Wind.* In the two exceptions the scene is still Monterey, but not Cannery Row, and the persons discussed appear nowhere else in the book.

The principal mythical theme of *Cannery Row* is the Logos, the Word made flesh. It is not a myth in the traditional meaning of the term; rather, it is a doctrine, religious and philosophical, Christian and pagan, which was used to interpret myth, and Steinbeck employs it in *Cannery Row* as he does genuine myths in other novels. The theme is stated in Chapter 2:

> The Word is a symbol and a delight which sucks up men and scenes, trees, plants, factories, and Pekinese. Then the Thing becomes the Word and back to Thing again, but warped and woven into a fantastic pattern. The Word sucks up Cannery Row, digests it and spews it out, and the Row has taken the shimmer of the green world and the sky-reflecting seas. Lee Chong is more than a Chinese grocer. He must be. Perhaps he is evil balanced and held suspended by good—an Asiatic planet held to its orbit by the pull of Lao Tze and held away from Lao Tze by the centrifugality of abacus and cash register—Lee Chong suspended, spinning, whirling among groceries and ghosts.

The author is a demiurge whose Word converts chaos into cosmos, the creative pattern which he imposes on the confusion of experience. The chaos is Cannery Row,

> a poem, a stink, a grating noise, a quality of light, a tone, a habit, a nostalgia, a dream. Cannery Row is the gathered and scattered, tin and iron and rust and splintered wood, chipped pavement and weedy lots and junk heaps, sardine canneries of corrugated iron, honky tonks, restaurants and whore houses, and little crowded groceries, and laboratories and flophouses.

Here are the elements that the author-demiurge sorts out for his creation: the Palace Flophouse, Doc's laboratory, Lee Chong's grocery, Dora's whorehouse (Bear Flag Restaurant), the La Ida barroom, the Hediondo Cannery, the vacant lot across from Doc's, the iron pipes in which men slept. The nondescript inhabitants whom a respectable citizen would call bums and whores become "the Virtues, the Graces, the Beauties," under the magic power of the Word.

"In the beginning was the Word," as in St. John's gospel; then Lee Chong, like John the Baptist, witness of the Word and the Light, prepared the way for the Virtues, Graces, and Beauties by acquiring the Abbeville shed, which became the Palace Flophouse and Grill when he turned it over to Mack and the boys. Like the Baptist standing between the Word and mankind's transgressions, Lee Chong stood between the Word of Lao Tze and the physical wants of Cannery Row. In his way he was a demiurge, too: on the chaos of goods in his store, "clothes, food, both fresh and canned, liquor, tobacco, fishing equipment, machinery, boats, cordage, caps, pork chops," he imposed his own order, as the author has imposed a personal order on Cannery Row.

The first eight chapters initiate and develop the theme of cosmos created from chaos by a demiurge through the agency of the Word. The author's Word has shaped the novel's Cannery Row; and this demiurge is a biologist who collects stories and puts them in his book as he collects marine animals and puts them into a bottle of sea water (so he tells us at the end of his prologue). Lee Chong's Word has determined the place and price of every article in his store. Dora Flood's Word has imposed order upon a disorderly house, which she named Bear Flag Restaurant. By giving the name Western Biological Laboratory to a confusion of

> sponges, tunicates, anemones, the stars and buttlestars, and sun stars, the bivalves, barnacles, the worms and shells, the fabulous and multiform little brothers, the living moving flowers of the sea, nudibranchs and tectibranchs, the spiked and nobbed and needly urchins, the crabs and demi-crabs, the little dragons, the snapping shrimps, . . . bugs and snails and spiders, and rattlesnakes, and rats, and honey bees and gila monsters

Doc has imposed order through his Word upon it. His Word, scientific terminology, has also given order to the "hurrying, fighting, feeding, breeding animals" of the Great Tide Pool. Mack's Word produced and organized the Palace Flophouse: his words "Kids might knock out the windows, you know . . . Place might burn down," and a promise of rent, induced Lee Chong to let him use the Abbeville shed. By giving a name to the shed and writing his friends' names on the floor, Mack brought order to a group of individualists. The Malloys moved into an abandoned boiler on a vacant lot full of weeds and junk and called it home; their fixed residence introduced order to the lot; Malloy was now a landlord who rented the pipes to men who wanted to sleep in them; to Mrs. Malloy the word "landlord" meant that she should have nice furniture and even curtains, although the boiler had no windows. The old Chinaman of Chapter IV, seen only at sunrise and sunset, is Demogorgon, above and behind everything; the word "Ching-Chong Chinaman" did not apply to him.

The Word starts the plot moving: first it is "That Doc is a fine fellow. We ought to do something for him," and then it is "celebrate," when Mack accused Hughie of imputing that condition to Doc:

> "Just because he doesn't run no dame naked through the streets in the daytime, you think Doc's celebrate."
> "What's celebrate?" Eddie asked.
> "That's when you can't get no dame," said Mack.
> "I thought it was a kind of a party," said Jones.
> A silence fell on the room. . . . Mack said, "Hum!"
> Eddie said, "What kind of a party you think Doc'd like?"
> "What other kind is there?" said Jones.

Doc's word that he needed frogs gave Mack's company the chance to earn the money needed for the party. After the abortive first party, Dora's simple words, "You gave him a party he didn't get to. Why don't you give him a party he does get to?" started movement towards the successful second party (then comes an interchapter in which Mary Talbot's word suffices to create parties). And Doc's word that October 27 was his birthday, although false, realized a party for him on the evening of that day.

The Word is truly creative, and the false word can be as powerful as the true, as Doc, who "loved true things," had learned through sad experience. The Word can create the appearance which hides reality. Dora's house had the appearance of being a restaurant. Dora had the name of madame, keeper of a house of sin, but was really a kindhearted philanthropist. Her man William had the name of watchman and was really a pimp; when he overheard Mack refer to him as a pimp, that word broke his heart and he committed suicide, giving reality to a word which the Greek cook considered only appearance:

"I hear like the fella talks about it don't never do it." Lee Chong called his surrender of the shed to Mack renting it and thus saved face; his wealth was perhaps "entirely in unpaid bills." But an IOU for eighty cents brought a stove to the Palace Flophouse. Doc, a real demiurge, could convert nonsense that he heard into a kind of wisdom. Hazel just liked to hear words spoken, to listen to the tone of conversation without absorbing the content. Mack was a master of words (though Doc's word vanquished Mack's at Red Williams' gas station when Mack tried to convert an order for gasoline into money). With judicious use of the word "Captain," praise of a dog, and a story about frogs needed for the study of cancer, Mack mollified a land-owner in the Carmel Valley and converted himself from trespasser into welcome guest and drinking companion. In truth, the Word is omnipresent in *Cannery Row* clear to the end, where Doc stops cleaning up the party mess to read from "Black Marigolds," a Sanskrit love poem (translated by E. Powys Mathers), in which the poet, listening to the

> . . . talking of wise men from towers
>
> . . .
>
> Found not the salt of the whispers of my girl,
>
> . . .
>
> Little wise words and little witty words,
> Wanton as water, honied with eagerness.

In such words one savors "the hot taste of life."

In contrast to the mythical theme, the organismic theme is underplayed in *Cannery Row*. We may, if we wish, think of the Palace Flophouse as an organism within the larger organism of Cannery Row, and that within the still larger organism of Monterey. But Steinbeck says little to suggest that these groups and communities are to be taken as single persons in themselves, apart from their members. Moods of gloom or joy pervade the Palace Flophouse and spread out to Cannery Row and all Monterey; news travels through the community in the usual mysterious way, and that is about all. Only the two parties are treated, facetiously, as organisms. The first was conceived in the word "celebrate"; its birth was mishandled; it had its moments of vitality, but was never really healthy. The second party, conceived in Dora's word, was properly nourished; people let the knowledge of it "grow gradually like a pupa in the cocoons of their imaginations"; and its life was lusty while it lasted. Steinbeck says,

> The nature of parties has been imperfectly studied. It is, however, generally understood that a party has a pathology, that it is a kind of an individual and that it is likely to be a very perverse individual. And it is also generally understood that a party hardly ever goes the way it is planned or intended.

It is the nature of the beast to have a short life.

> No one has studied the psychology of a dying party. It may be raging, howling, boiling, and then a fever sets in and a little silence and then quickly quickly it is gone, the guests go home or go to sleep or wander away to some other affair and they leave a dead body.

Facetious—but the life history of the parties is the central thread of *Cannery Row* and has a subtle significance, as we shall see in a moment.

If the group organism is comparatively slighted, ecology remains a fruitful source of interpretation and imagery. When we first see Doc in action, he is collecting specimens in the Great Tide Pool near Monterey. It is a microcosm of creatures, "fantastic with hurrying, fighting, feeding, breeding animals." Crabs, starfish, nudibranchs, eels, shrimps, seductive and deadly anemones, octopuses, barnacles, and limpets live in it, feeding on one another in an unending series, or consuming another's waste products. Predatory, symbiotic, and parasitic animals live together in lusty profusion. The tide pool is Steinbeck's central image in *Cannery Row*. The Row is a tide pool of cannery workers and managers, bums, whores, storekeepers, and Doc; here, too, are parasites and commensals and predators. It is not only a corner of the tide pool of Monterey, but also an image of the whole world as tide pool: "[the Row's] inhabitants are . . . Everybody," for this book is a kind of morality play.

> Mack and the boys . . . are the Virtues, the Graces, the Beauties of the hurried mangled craziness of Monterey and the cosmic Monterey where men in fear and hunger destroy their stomachs in the fight to secure certain food, where men hungering for love destroy everything lovable about them. . . . In the world ruled by tigers with ulcers, rutted by strictured bulls, scavenged by blind jackals, Mack and the boys dine delicately with the tigers, fondle the frantic heifers, and wrap up the crumbs to feed the sea gulls of Cannery Row. What can it profit a man to gain the whole world and to come to his prop-

erty with a gastric ulcer, a blown prostate, and bifocals? Mack and the boys avoid the trap, walk around the poison, step over the noose . . .

Doc developed the morality theme when he talked to Richard Frost about Mack's company:

"I think they survive in this particular world better than other people. In a time when people tear themselves to pieces with ambition and nervousness and covetousness, they are relaxed. All of our so-called successful men are sick men, with bad stomachs, and bad souls, but Mack and the boys are healthy and curiously clean. They can do what they want. They can satisfy their appetites without calling them something else."

That is the philosophy of *Tortilla Flat,* too, but in the same conversation it becomes mixed with the social Darwinism of *Sea of Cortez.* In almost the words of that book, Doc tells Richard that the virtues like kindness, generosity, and honesty "are the concomitants of failure in our system," and the vices like greed, meanness, and acquisitiveness "are the traits of success"; and while men admire the virtues, they love the products of the vices. Yet we gather that Mack's company have these virtues and shun these vices, and are nevertheless more successful at living than the greedy and acquisitive. Here, however, Steinbeck says "failure in our system" and does not express the idea in terms of survival and extinction, as in *Sea of Cortez.* He is therefore opposing a cosmic reality to the appearance of success and failure in a transitory system.

Steinbeck also reveals a deeper reality behind the appearance of success and happiness in Mack's mode of life. After the disastrous party, Mack said to Doc, "It don't do no good to say I'm sorry. I been sorry all my life. This ain't no new thing. It's always like this. . . . I had a wife . . . Same thing. Ever'thing I done turned sour. . . . If I done a good thing it got poisoned up some way." Still this is the Mack who is "healthy and curiously clean," and who "has qualities of genius." Behind the idyllic picture of pleasant loafers we glimpse the maladjustment which brings a man to Skid Row, where he spends his time cadging money to buy bottles of cheap wine or liquor. It is not really a pleasant street to live on, not even in Monterey. Steinbeck betrays the truth almost inadvertently, for, if clearly seen, it would spoil the point that he wants to make.

He is attacking and satirizing the drive for success, as commonly conceived, as wealth, ownership, status. Set against that is loafing, ultimately unsatisfactory; scientific work, which is lonely; and splendid moments of pleasure, "the hot taste of life," which soon vanish. The dominant commercial values are part of nature's order; the author does not probe the society which produces them. The canneries are barely visible in the background. At the outset we see the working day begin as managers and workers flock into Cannery Row; but we are told that the work day interrupts the Row's normal life, which returns when the canneries close for the night. We hear once of the cannery companies' greed for profits. Otherwise they are places that provide temporary jobs for the Flophouse boys, junk for the vacant lot, and fish heads for cats.

The acquisitive society simply is, and there is no remedy except for the individual who can escape into idleness or creative activity or fun. This is the outcome of dubious battle. Mack of *Cannery Row* looks like a deliberate burlesque of Mac of *In Dubious Battle,* and through the power of the Word the Party is rendered innocuous. Each Mac[k] stands in complementary relation to Doc; each is a man of devices, and Doc is the objective non-teleological observer (biologist Doc also practices medicine in a small way). Both Docs are lonely men, and a character says of each that he needs a woman. The most striking parallel occurs when each Mac[k] tactfully admires a landowner's pointer in order to win the owner's favor and gain access to the land for his group. Both Mac[k]s express a wish to have one of the pointer's pups. Both enter with their men upon the land to promote the good of a party. The difference between the parties of the two books reflects the shift in Steinbeck's attitude to social problems: the Party is definitely rejected and we are invited to a party. In *Cannery Row,* this change is symbolized in the scene at the landowner's house: the "captain" condemns his wife, an Assemblywoman very active in politics (that is, in her Party), in her absence; he and the boys have a drinking bout, which messes up her orderly house. The land is no longer used for a doomed strikers' camp, but for an uproariously successful frog hunt, which will earn money for the party. This is the kind of party to join, we are told. Our sad, lonely condition can be alleviated only by moments of great joy, parties, and love affairs, when we savor "the hot taste of life"; afterwards—melancholy and "Black Marigolds." That is the Word spoken to us in *Cannery Row.*

THE WAYWARD BUS

Early in 1947 *The Wayward Bus,* the first Steinbeck novel written in the post-war period, was published. The action takes place on a single day of early spring between Rebel Corners and San Juan de la Cruz, fictitious localities at the eastern and western ends of an imaginary county road which connects two north-south highways in California. Juan Chicoy's bus, making a daily round trip, carries Greyhound passengers between the valley and coast routes. The bus is a device, in the "Grand Hotel" style, to bring together a motley collection of persons, who interact for a few hours and then go their separate ways. Juan, who keeps a service station and lunchroom at Rebel Corners, has eight passengers: Mr. Pritchard, a wealthy businessman, on his way to Mexico with his wife and his daughter Mildred; Camille Oaks, a stripper who exudes sex appeal (Steinbeck's most seductive woman since La Santa Roja); Ernest Horton, a gadget salesman; Van Brunt, a disagreeable old man, due to have a stroke; Norma, a simple-minded young waitress who has a crush on Clark Gable; and Juan's helper, the adolescent Pimples Carson, whose "concupiscence was constant" and whose "cheeks were rivuleted and rotted and eroded with acne." Back at the Corners, Juan's wife, Alice, goes on a terrific binge.

The county road crossed the San Ysidro River twice, where the stream made a great loop; and on this day the river waters had risen enough to endanger the poorly constructed bridges. Juan did not want to get caught inside the loop, and so took an old dirt road that went around it. There the bus bogged down in mud; Juan left it, ostensibly to get help, but really intending to abandon his wife and business and run away to Mexico. In his absence the tensions that had been building up all day among the passengers found various expressions. After dallying with Mildred Pritchard in a barn down the road, Juan came back, freed the bus, and drove it on to San Juan.

This too is a morality, and it has for epigraph the first six lines of *Everyman*. Yet the old "morall playe" has not shaped the plot or structure of *The Wayward Bus*. We can only say that the bus represents the world, whose inhabitants journey toward death (San Juan de la Cruz, reached at night, when the town's lights shine in the distance as if those of the heavenly city). "In worldlye ryches is all theyr mynde"—money, position, Hollywood glamor, cosmetics. On the cliff above the stalled bus is painted the word "Repent." Van Brunt, who suffers his fatal stroke on the way, is Death in person. He insists on making the trip with the others; at the first bridge he refuses to stay behind, though he points out the certain dangers of going ahead by either road; it is he who first indicates the roundabout road which they take and which finally reaches the same destination. But although Camille might be identified with Beauty and Pimples with Five Wits, the other passengers cannot be convincingly paired with *Everyman* characters. Juan Chicoy's initials indicate that he represents Jesus Christ, who came back to rescue the troubled world that he wanted to abandon; for Juan was also, as Steinbeck said, "all the god the fathers you ever saw driving a . . . battered world through time and space." On his dashboard sat a small metal image of the Virgin of Guadalupe, his confidante and "connection with eternity." "This dark Virgin was his mother," who had made the Guadalupana "her own personal goddess." Juan is a non-teleological deity, wedded to the very teleological Alice and carrying a load of teleological passengers.

The front-bumper palimpsest, "Sweetheart" painted over the barely visible "el Gran Poder de Jesus," symbolizes the contrast between appearance and reality which the story is intended to point up. Pimples loves sweet cakes and pies; Mrs. Pritchard is known to her friends as a sweet woman; Van Brunt eats canned peaches and drinks the sweet juice; after finishing her whisky Alice Chicoy consumes port wine; Horton sells toys; nearly everyone is committed to the sweet life pictured in movies, magazines, and advertisements. But beneath the sweetness we see disease, frustration, lust, meanness, deceit, ugliness, death. The passengers speak rules, formulas, clichés, of health and morality, which are in themselves bogus. Only Juan Chicoy looks objectively at his desires and knows them for what they are.

Yet Juan is hardly a convincing character. His streak of cruelty seems more believable than his superior objectivity. When he first stirred Mildred, she thought that she saw "a cruel, leering triumph in his face." But his transcendent role obscures these credible touches of earthiness. We have a realistic story told as a morality of Everyman; but though the narrative skill displayed is great, vehicle and tenor do not jibe. We seem to have a critique of middle-class America: Mr. and Mrs. Pritchard are pilloried without mercy. Yet Steinbeck appears to waver between a limited critique of contemporary bourgeois society and a comprehensive critique of the human condition. It turns out to be hardly one or the other; we have neither Babbitt nor Everyman.

The biological interpretation of human society is no longer prominent. The passenger group is barely visible as a single organism. At first charged with tensions, the group relaxed as a unit with laughter after Pritchard's fall into Camille's lap, which caused his wife to ask him whether he was "trying to sit in that lady's lap?"; then "Some chemical association was formed." And Pritchard is completely group-man, merely "a unit in a corporation, a unit in a club, in a lodge, in a church, in a political party." The ecological image is changed from tide pool to roadside ditch, where between road and fence grew tall mustard plants (in which birds made nests), wild turnips, poppies, thistles, milkweeds, water cress, and all sorts of weeds.

> The ditches beside the road under the high growth of weeds became the home of weasels and bright-colored water snakes, and the drinking places for birds in the evening. The meadow larks sat all morning on the old fences in the spring and whistled their yodeling song. And the wild doves sat on the barbed wire in the evening . . . , and their call rang down the miles in a sustained note. At evening the night hawks coursed along the ditches, looking for meat, and in the dark the barn owls searched for rabbits. And when a cow was sick the great ugly turkey buzzards sat on the old fence waiting for death.

The ditch is the symbolic correlative of the bus and of the world. The buzzards are Van Brunt, waiting for death; the doves, birds of Aphrodite and Ishtar, suggest Camille, whose voiceless call stirs the men passengers and affects the women too; the hawks and owls represent the human predators—Pritchard, Pimples, Horton—hunting for money or women or both. Whereas in *Cannery Row* we never forget the tide pool, the roadside ditch almost escapes notice in *The Wayward Bus:* it is introduced, described, and then is all but abandoned.

THE PEARL

The Pearl was published by Viking Press in November, 1947, about ten months after *The Wayward Bus*, although it had been written in the winter of 1944–45 and had appeared in the *Woman's Home Companion* of December, 1945. It is a novelette expanded from a folktale of Lower California which Steinbeck had reported in *Sea of Cortez* as a true story of a typical event that had "happened at La Paz in recent years":

> An Indian boy by accident found a pearl of great size, an unbelievable pearl. He knew its value was so great that he need never work again. In his one pearl he had the ability to be drunk as long as he wished, to marry any one of a number of girls, and to make many more a little happy too. In his great pearl lay salvation, for he could in advance purchase masses sufficient to pop him out of Purgatory like

a squeezed watermelon seed. In addition he could shift a number of dead relatives a little nearer to Paradise.

But every broker to whom he took the pearl offered him so little for it that he refused to sell it and hid it under a stone. That night and the next he was attacked and beaten and searched; fleeing inland, he was waylaid and tortured. Then in the dark, he "skulked like a hunted fox to the beach," took the pearl from under the stone, and cast it into the sea.

In the novelette the story is no longer a picaresque yarn but a pathetic narrative of serious intent. Kino, finder of "the Pearl of the World," wanted to buy fine new clothes, a new harpoon, and a rifle; to send his boy, Coyotito, to school; and to have a church wedding with Juana, his common-law wife. When he fled the attacks made on him in town, he took the pearl with him; and Juana, carrying Coyotito, accompanied him to the hills. Relentless trackers came after them. Kino finally killed his pursuers, one of whom had killed Coyotito when he fired a rifle up the mountainside. Then Kino and Juana walked openly and silently in broad daylight back to town and through the streets to the beach, where Kino threw the great pearl back into the water.

It is another morality, a "black-and-white story like a parable," as Steinbeck called it. He has magnified the simple moral of the Mexican tale by transforming the anecdote into a Hymn of the Soul. For, as Thomas Sugrue has perceived, Steinbeck surely had in mind the Hymn of the Soul or Pearl from the Gnostic Acts of Judas Thomas. But once more the myth is inverted. In the Gnostic hymn the prince (the soul), whom his royal (heavenly) parents sent to fetch "the one pearl, / Which is in the midst of the sea / Hard by the loud-breathing serpent," tarried among the treacherous Egyptians (this world) and forgot his mission, until a message from his parents recalled him to his duty; then he took the pearl and went home to his inheritance. Kino, however, taking the pearl that promised salvation, rejected it and returned to familiar and comfortable poverty. Having said, "This pearl has become my soul . . . If I give it up I shall lose my soul," he did give it up. For he encountered the treacherous Egyptians after finding the Pearl of the World; and the pearl of salvation became damnation for Kino. It was an ambiguous treasure, both Grail and Nibelung gold.

The Pearl is a morality set to music. It opens with the Song of the

Family, as Kino awakened at dawn in his hut, soon countered by the Song of Evil, accompanied by Juana's Hail Marys, when a scorpion advanced on Coyotito and stung him, becoming the Song of the Enemy roaring in Kino's ears as he stamped the scorpion to death. After a lull the music of the enemy pounded in his ears when he knocked at the doctor's gate. Then when Kino dived into the sea to find pearls, that he might have money to pay the doctor, the Song of the Undersea beat within him, and in its counter-melody "was the Song of the Pearl That Might Be." Then Kino found the great pearl and at once "the secret melody of the maybe pearl broke clear and beautiful," and as he imagined all the goods that the pearl would bring him, "the music of the pearl rose like a chorus of trumpets in his ears." And so it goes: the music or song of the family, of the pearl, of evil and the enemy, oppose, underlie, and succeed one another, rising or falling according to the action. At the end the Song of the Family rang fierce in Kino's ears; the music of the pearl became distorted and insane, and at last, "drifted to a whisper and disappeared." There the symphony comes to an end; we do not hear the Song of the Family going on alone. For though events have come full circle, they are not just as they were before: Kino has lost his son, his house, and his canoe.

. What then is the moral of this drama, the meaning of this parable? In his prologue Steinbeck says, "If this story is a parable, perhaps everyone takes his own meaning from it and reads his own life into it." The statement must be as true of Steinbeck as of anyone. Surely we may suppose that the pearl represents that accumulation of wealth and property which is depreciated in Steinbeck's earlier novels in favor of the simple life of few wants. And yet what Kino wants is not luxury and riches, but more advantages for himself and his family, a better return for his labor. That is what the pearl offers him and what he throws away with the pearl. And the narrator tells us that it is quite proper for a man to increase his wants: ". . . it is one of the greatest talents the species has and one that has made it superior to animals that are satisfied with what they have." The narrator also tells us that we must be tactful with the gods, who "do not love men's plans, and . . . do not love success unless it comes by accident." It looks as if we were once more being taught the lesson of *Cup of Gold* and *Of Mice and Men,* the vanity of human wishes: our goals may be fine, but we just cannot reach them. May we suppose that Kino's woes have their source in the market system? We get a good look at the pearl buyers, who are really "only one pearl buyer with many hands," a kind of collective organism, whose main purpose is to cheat the pearl fishers. But no; they are only men doing their job as well as they can. The fishermen are not meant to prosper. Once they thought of organizing and of hiring an agent to take their pearls directly to the capital and sell them. But after two agents absconded with the pearls, they gave up, and the priest drew the moral: the fishermen's loss was God's punishment upon them for trying to leave their station. Is this irony, directed at the Church? Kino's brother observed that Kino had defied "not the pearl buyers, but the whole structure, the whole way of life, . . ." And one cannot successfully challenge that structure: it is not the economic system but the universe. Juana knew that Kino would hurl his strength against a mountain, and "that the mountain would stand while the man broke himself." We may suppose that Kino's assailants and trackers are sent by the pearl buyers and greedy doctor. Still they are dark, never clearly seen, mysterious, as if Pepé's invisible pursuers in "Flight" were one with the dark watchers. And Kino went back to his station, having lost everything because he had not been satisfied with what he had.

Steinbeck professed to be telling a teleological tale in *The Pearl:* "And, as with all retold tales . . . , there are only good and bad things and black and white things and good and evil things and no in-between anywhere." On the contrary, everything in *The Pearl* is in-between. Who or what is pure good or evil, black or white, except possibly the doctor (evil and black)? And he too had his dreams of going back to a pleasant life in Paris. This is a non-teleological parable: this is the way things are.

As one might expect in a tale that grew out of *Sea of Cortez,* Steinbeck's interest in biology is more evident than in his other novels of the forties. Here is the town that "is a thing like a colonial animal," which "has a whole emotion," and through which news travels swiftly by mysterious channels. The news of Kino's pearl "stirred up something infinitely black and evil in the town; the black distillate was like the scorpion . . . The poison sacs of the town began to manufacture venom, and the town swelled and puffed with the pressure of it." The town as organism is plainly Leviathan, who will root out any troublesome member. And in the town as ecological unit each kind of inhabitant—pearl fishers, pearl buyers, Spanish aristocrats, beggars, ants, dogs—has its niche, its particular means of preserving itself. And each individual must stay within the niche of his kind and not encroach on another's.

BURNING BRIGHT

In the summer of 1950 Steinbeck completed his third experiment in the play-novelette form. He called it *Burning Bright,* taking for epigraph the first stanza of Blake's "Tyger." The story is meant to celebrate the miracle of life: despite man's cruelty, violence, weakness, and wickedness, some life force has framed him in "fearful symmetry." It was consciously intended to be another *Everyman;* its universal meaning is emphasized by changing the characters, who keep the same names and carry forward a single plot, from circus people in the first act to farmers in the second and seamen in the third. In the final short scene they are faceless, wearing surgical masks in a maternity ward, now apparently of any or every occupation. In the first act Joe Saul says to Friend Ed: "I know it is a thing that can happen to anyone in any place and time—a farmer or a sailor, or a lineless, faceless Everyone!" And Steinbeck said about it that "The attempt was to lift the story to the parable expression of the morality plays."

The central theme is Joe Saul's sterility, of which he did not become certain until the third act. Neither of two wives had borne him a child, and he was now fifty, married for two years to Mordeen, a young woman—a happy marriage marred only by her failure to become a mother. Like Joseph Wayne in *To a God Unknown,* Joe Saul believed that he was not carrying out his duty to be fertile and reproduce his kind. To preserve the marriage and Joe Saul's happiness, Mordeen allowed Victor, Joe Saul's assistant—a hardboiled, insensitive, townbred boy—to have his way with her, selecting him for purely eugenic reasons, since she disliked his character. She intended that the child be Joe Saul's, and Joe Saul thought that the child was really his. But Victor was not easily pushed aside; although he revealed nothing to Joe Saul, he constantly importuned Mordeen to leave her husband. When he became too troublesome (as a seaman on shipboard in the third act), Friend Ed—who understood everything—quietly hit Victor over the head and pushed him overboard. Joe Saul, having learned the truth, successfully overcame his hateful feelings and gladly accepted Mordeen's son as his own, saying, "I had to walk into the black to know—to know that every man is father to all children and every child must have all men as father."

Steinbeck thus once more states the thesis that all life is holy. Again it is not the individual life that matters but the life of the species, in which every unit participates in every other. Although eccentricity and individuality leaven the collective organism, they

115

must be consistent with group unity: Victor was a disruptive force that had to be destroyed. His alien quality is emphasized in every act: he did not belong. He was competent, but lacked Joe Saul's inbred feeling for his craft, inherited from ancestors who had been performers, farmers, sailors, for generations. Each craft community or guild, a collective organism which expels troublesome alien elements, represents the whole species.

It is all rather hard on Victor, the only character who experiences growth, changing from a tough selfishness to love for another and admirable self-restraint, when he refrains from blurting out the truth to Joe Saul. True enough, Joe Saul overcomes his bitterness and hate, but his character does not really change; he simply has a more expansive wisdom at the end. The propositions that "all that lives is holy," and that all men are brothers, do not include Victor, it seems. Why, one wonders, should Victor be underprivileged and not have the right to life, love, and parenthood that is granted to Joe Saul? In fact, the moral issue that Victor's role raises is evaded by putting Victor out of the way. It is hardly satisfactory to be told that Victor is not really dead, but lives on in his son and in every man.

"This is *the Child*," Joe Saul said to Mordeen. Joe Saul is both Joseph, husband of Mary, and Saul, first king of Israel. Victor is David, a comely young man, whose harp music could dispel Saul's dark moods, as Victor's talents removed the poison from Joe Saul's spirit. Nature was with Victor, as the Lord with David. The course of Joe Saul's relations with Victor recalls that of King Saul's with David. The older man was often jealous of the younger and wanted to kill him; he struck him (Joe Saul struck Victor) or tried to (Saul threw a javelin at David); he became reconciled when he learned that his rival had spared him (Victor saved Joe Saul's line). David was victor; but Victor's victory was also Joe Saul's and Everyman's. So the story of Saul and David served Steinbeck in *Burning Bright* as it served Thomas Hardy in *The Mayor of Casterbridge*. It is the archetype of tales of rivalry between an older and a younger man.

The reader may accept the general thesis of *Burning Bright*, that all men are brothers, but is likely to feel disappointed with this statement of it. He remains troubled by the fate of Victor, who is hardly treated as a brother. The parable, therefore, does not ring true, and its unsoundness is enhanced by Steinbeck's attempt at "parable expression" in the characters' speeches, which only succeeds in being sentimental and unreal. Unlike *Of Mice and Men* and *The Moon Is*

Down, this play-novelette found little favor among either readers or theatre-goers.

Steinbeck wrote three books of nonfiction during the 1940's. *Bombs Away* (1942) is an account of the training of a bomber crew, written for the Army Air Corps to acquaint the public with its program. In 1943 Steinbeck spent several months in Europe and North Africa as special correspondent of the New York *Herald Tribune,* which published from June to December a series of articles that he wrote on the attitudes and activities of American soldiers; the series was finally published in book form, entitled *Once There Was a War,* in 1958. In 1947 Steinbeck made a trip to Soviet Russia with the photographer Robert Capa, and his account of it, illustrated by Capa's pictures, appeared in April, 1948, as *A Russian Journal.* These books, although pleasant reading, add nothing to Steinbeck's stature and are not significant, as was *Sea of Cortez,* for an understanding of his fiction. Therefore I refer the reader to the terminal Selected Bibliography for brief comments on them.

9

⪦ EAST OF EDEN AND AFTER

IN THE forties Steinbeck was clearly turning his principal interest from biology and sociology to individual ethics. He was one of several writers whom the Second World War and its aftermath made aware of the "problem of evil." Hence his deliberate attempt to write novels that would also be moralities, culminating in 1950 with *Burning Bright*. In *East of Eden,* published in September of 1952, he completed the transition; it is a lengthy treatment of man's capacity for both good and evil. In it Steinbeck "plainly announces . . . that it is as a moralist that he wants to be taken," as Joseph Wood Krutch expressed it.

EAST OF EDEN

Fourteen years earlier, when he had finished writing *The Grapes of Wrath,* Steinbeck wrote in his journal that he must some day write a book about his own people. In 1947 he started work upon a book that he called "Salinas Valley," which would be the story of the Hamiltons, his mother's family. Early in the drafting he introduced a fictitious second family, the Trasks, whose role expanded to the point of taking over the novel; and in 1951 the title was changed to *East of Eden.* The finished novel is still two stories, the Trasks and the Hamiltons, or rather three: the story of Cathy Ames is really a separate strand that becomes entwined with the central Trask story in one phase only; thereafter it goes its own way, a parallel strand that comes occasionally into important contact with the Trask strand. The Hamilton story is a subordinate and independent strand that barely touches the other two: the Hamiltons have almost nothing to do with Cathy and little to do with the Trasks. The Trask story needs Cathy Ames, but not the Hamiltons, who can be dropped out without affecting the Trask story at all.

The novel has four Parts. In the first (1862–1900) the three stories are begun, and the Trask and Cathy stories are developed until Adam Trask marries Cathy. Part Two (1900–1902) brings the Trasks and Hamiltons together in the Salinas Valley, ending with the naming of Cathy's twins, after she has abandoned them and her husband and become a whore (called Kate) in Salinas; and her story is carried to the point where by devious means she acquired ownership of the brothel in which she worked. In Part Three (1911–12) the Hamilton story moves forward on its own from the last days of Samuel Hamilton to its conclusion in the deaths of Dessie and Tom Hamilton, while the Trask story marks time (Adam Trask becomes half alive after ten years of spiritual coma), and Cathy is all but absent. Part Four (1912–18) is the story of Adam Trask and his sons after they had moved from the Trask ranch to Salinas; the parallel Cathy-Kate story ends with her suicide; and the Hamilton story is touched upon only in Will Hamilton's role as Cal Trask's partner in a bean brokerage. The central narrative throughout is the fictional biography of Adam Trask from his birth in the second year of the Civil War until his death in the last year of World War I. Five short chapters (three of these are introductions to the Parts) present the historical and moral contexts of the Trask and Hamilton stories in fulfillment of the author's promise to write the story of his family and country. The design and magnitude of *East of Eden,* and Steinbeck's own remarks about it, indicate that it was meant to be a climactic work, his greatest achievement, for which every earlier book was practice. But few Steinbeck readers will place it higher than *The Grapes of Wrath;* the majority may see it as a second peak in his career, but not nearly so high as the first.

Although morality has now nearly eclipsed biology as a formative principle in Steinbeck's fiction, his biological knowledge still makes an occasional appearance and remains an important source of metaphor and simile. For example, the vicious Cathy Ames was a psychic monster, produced by "a twisted gene or a malformed egg." But the group organism, prominent in earlier novels, has almost disappeared from view. It is employed in only a few instances. The army is depicted as a group that tolerates no individual differences in its members, absorbing them completely into itself. Lee, the Trasks' sage Chinese servant, used as a spokesman by the author, says that a family is something hard to root out, once it has dug into the earth and scratched out a home. Towns like Salinas are described as having an occasional "mild eructation of morality," which results in raids on gambling joints. That is about all—statements that another novelist might have made, and which would require no notice here had not Steinbeck established the organismic theme in earlier novels. In fact, in one moralizing section, the concept of the group, because it is hostile to "the free, exploring mind of the individual," is rejected in favor of "the individual mind and spirit of a man," which is the only "creative instrument"; the group never creates anything. Leviathan is cast into outer darkness. *East of Eden* does not deal with groups, aside from families—and not even the Hamilton family looks like a single organism.

The mythical vehicle of Steinbeck's moral message is the story of Cain and Abel, as the title indicates. And in this novel Steinbeck is not content with a subtle suggestion of the myth, but must make sure that his readers will not miss it. In Chapter 22 Samuel Hamilton reads Genesis 4:1–16 aloud to Adam Trask and Lee, and the three men discuss it thoroughly on two occasions. The principal characters of the Trask-Cathy story have names beginning with A or C. The Abel characters are Adam, Aaron (Aron), and Alice Trask, Mr. and Mrs. Ames, and Abra Bacon; the Cain characters are Cyrus, Charles, and Caleb (Cal) Trask, and Cathy Ames. After Adam's sons were born Samuel Hamilton said, "He'll bring in a crop of candy canes."

The Cain-and-Abel story is enacted in two generations of the Trask family. Adam and Charles were half-brothers, sons of Cyrus Trask, a Union soldier in the Civil War. Cyrus loved his elder son Adam more than he loved Charles. On his birthday Cyrus received gifts from his sons and preferred Adam's gift, a stray mongrel pup, to the fine pocketknife which Charles gave him after earning the money to buy it by cutting and selling a load of wood. Thus herdsman Abel's gift (a domestic animal, guardian of flocks) was preferred to farmer Cain's (a product of a farmer's labor). In a jealous rage Charles beat Adam nearly to death. In "The Sons of Cyrus Trask" (*Collier's,* July 12, 1952), a separate treatment of this episode as a short story, Steinbeck has Cyrus shoot Charles to death after the beating; but in the novel, although Cyrus sought Charles with a gun, he failed to find him and his anger eventually cooled. Charles stayed on the family farm in Connecticut, where one day he

injured his forehead so badly that a large scar was left on it. Adam
went into the cavalry (a herdsman role) at his father's insistence.

After ten years in the army and more years wandering across the
country, Adam was living with Charles on the Trask farm when
Cathy Ames crawled to their door, terribly beaten by the whoremaster Edwards. Adam fell in love with her while nursing her, and
married her, obstinately refusing to inquire into her past. Cathy was
the sort of person who would put sleeping medicine in Adam's tea
on her wedding night so that she could enter Charles's bed; and she
appears to have been impregnated by both brothers, for she bore non-
identical twins, one of whom (Caleb) looked like Charles and was
like Charles in nature. Contrary to the Biblical story, it was Adam
(Abel), not Charles (Cain), who left the family land and went west
to California, where the twins were born and Cathy deserted him.
There he became the first Adam who lost his Eden (a happy life with
Cathy and his children on excellent farm land in the Salinas Valley)
and was father of Cain (Caleb) and Abel (Aaron). Adam preferred
his son Aaron (later spelled Aron), who in boyhood raised Belgian
hares (the herdsman role); the less likeable Caleb (Cal) wanted to
be a farmer. When he was seventeen, Cal, in partnership with Will
Hamilton, contracted for bean crops to sell to the British Purchasing
Agency; he made $15,000 and gave it to his father, who had suf-
fered severe losses in a business venture. Adam cruelly refused Cal's
gift on the ground that the money was war profit, unfairly gained,
and invidiously compared it to Aron's success in entering Stanford
one year early: "I would have been so happy if you could have given
me—well, what your brother has—pride in the thing he's doing,
gladness in his progress. Money, even clean money, doesn't stack up
with that." This is Jehovah's speech to Cain (Genesis 4:7), as Sam
Hamilton interpreted it: "I don't like this. Try again. Bring me
something I like and I'll set you up alongside your brother." Cal
got revenge by taking Aron to watch the "circus" at Kate's whorehouse and revealing to him that Kate was their mother (Cal had discovered this some time before). Aron, a pure boy who had intended
to enter the Episcopal ministry, was profoundly shocked, as Cal had
expected, since the knowledge shattered Aron's unreal image of an
angelic mother who had died in his infancy. The very next morning
Aron enlisted in the army, soon was sent to France, and died in action. On the day of Aron's enlistment, Adam asked Cal where his
brother was, and Cal replied, "How do I know? . . . Am I supposed to look after him?"

Steinbeck, of course, puts more into the story than can be found in Genesis 4, which says nothing about either brother's attitude towards Adam. The irony of the fathers' partiality in *East of Eden* is that neither Adam nor Aron loved his father, whereas Charles loved Cyrus and Cal loved Adam, and each tried hard to please his father. Again, Steinbeck introduces rivalry over a woman into both generations of brothers, more obscurely in the first, since Charles disliked Cathy; but he did admit her to his bed and left her half his fortune when he died. In the next generation Abra, Aron's boyhood sweetheart, transferred her love to Cal after Aron's enlistment. Steinbeck read a good deal about Genesis while writing *East of Eden* and probably came upon a later Jewish legend (current before 300 A.D.) which elaborates the brief and bare scriptural narrative: both Cain and Abel had a twin sister, each intended to become her twin's wife and so ensure the survival of mankind. Abel's twin sister was so beautiful that Cain wanted her; therefore he picked a quarrel with Abel, killed him, and married Abel's twin, that mysterious wife of Cain who bore his son Enoch in the land of Nod (Genesis 4:17).

Furthermore, Steinbeck had to fuse Adam and Jehovah in one person, Cyrus Trask in the first generation, Adam Trask in the second. Cathy is a fusion of Eve, the Eden serpent, and Cain's wife—the beating which the whoremaster gave her had left a scar on her forehead. Steinbeck emphasizes her serpent nature by giving her a heart-shaped face, an abnormally small mouth, a little pointed tongue that sometimes flicked around her lips, small sharp teeth with the canine teeth longer and more pointed than the others, tiny ears without lobes and pressed close to her head, unblinking eyes, narrow hips. She liked the dark and shunned light. When Sam Hamilton delivered her twins, she snarled at him with lips drawn up from her teeth and bit his hand severely. Since Steinbeck accepts the Christian identification of the Eden snake with Satan, he also represents Cathy as a devil: "There was a time when a girl like Cathy would have been called possessed by the devil." Drink turned her into a deadly demon. She had small round feet "like little hoofs," her mouth corners turned up a little, and her body was boyish.

The Eden theme becomes explicit in Adam's stated purpose of founding a family seat on a ranch in the Salinas Valley: "Look, Samuel, I mean to make a garden of my land. Remember my name is Adam. So far I've had no Eden, let alone been driven out." And Samuel asked, "Where will the orchard be?" adding a moment later, ". . . Eves delight in apples." Both Adam and Sam shared the dream of all settlers in the Salinas Valley, that there the American earthly paradise would be realized; but Sam felt a sinister influence too: "There's a blackness on this valley. . . . It's as though some old ghost haunted it out of the dead ocean below and troubled the air with unhappiness." Drilling a well for Adam he struck a meteorite; this "shooting star that fell a million years ago" is Lucifer, the fallen angel, and symbolizes the lurking evil in the valley, where Cathy had come to live.

The story of Cain and Abel, Lee said to Adam and Sam, "is the symbol story of the human soul," "the best-known story in the world because it is everybody's story." The three men found the story perplexing when they first discussed it. Ten years later, when they had gathered for the last time, Lee had cleared up the difficulties with the help of four aged Chinese sages, who had studied Hebrew for just this purpose. They solved the problem of Genesis 4:7, as given in the King James version, "And unto thee shall be his desire, and thou shalt rule over him," by translating the verb form *timshol* (not *timshel* as Steinbeck has it) "thou mayest rule" instead of "thou shalt rule"; and they took "sin" as antecedent of the masculine pronouns. This, Lee said in triumph, "was the gold from our mining": the translation "thou shalt rule" implies predestination; "do thou rule," as in the American Standard version, orders a man to master sin; but "thou mayest rule" gives a man a choice: he can master sin if he wants to. " 'Thou mayest,' " Lee said, "might be the most important word in the world," for "that makes a man great, . . . for in his weakness and his filth and his murder of his brother he has still the great choice."

This, then, is the message of *East of Eden,* a message that many can accept, even though those who "love true things" must reject Lee's interpretation of Genesis 4:7. That verse has an obviously corrupt text, and the sentence at issue appears to be out of place. For one thing, the masculine pronouns cannot refer to "sin," which translates a Hebrew feminine noun. And *timshol* will not bear the meaning which Steinbeck puts upon it. He apparently read or was told that the Hebrew imperfect tense, which indicates incomplete action at any time, is used where English employs either the vivid future tense (*will, shall*) or the potential (*would, should, may, might*); in either case the action is unfulfilled. If a translation as potential suited this verse, it would be simply "you would rule"; it cannot be a permissive "may." Steinbeck, furthermore, constantly translates *timshol* "thou mayest," dropping "rule," as if the Hebrew form were simply an auxiliary. Many a sermon, however, has drawn a fine meaning from a faulty translation of a corrupt text.

According to Lee, the story of Cain and Abel is important because it is a story of rejection, from which all evil flows, since "with rejection comes anger, and with anger some kind of crime in revenge for the rejection, and with the crime guilt—and there is the story of mankind." Or as the author states it in a moralizing chapter (34), "most of . . . [men's] vices are attempted short cuts to love." In the same chapter Steinbeck tells us that his story has the same subject as every other story:

> I believe that there is one story in the world, and only one, . . .
> Humans are caught—in their lives, in their thoughts, in their hungers and ambitions, in their avarice and cruelty, and in their kindness and generosity too—in a net of good and evil........................
> We have only one story. All novels, all poetry, are built on the never-ending contest in ourselves of good and evil.

As Krutch has pointed out, for Steinbeck as moralist good and evil are absolute and objective. We have come a long way, it seems, from Jim Casy's doctrine in *The Grapes of Wrath* that "There ain't no sin and there ain't no virtue. There's just stuff people do," and from Doc Burton's refusal in *In Dubious Battle* "to put on the blinders of 'good' and 'bad,'" because they would limit his vision and destroy his objectivity. And it seems to me that Steinbeck has limited his vision in *East of Eden*.

The reader is never clear about the relation of good to evil in this novel, for it is presented in four inconsistent ways. (1) Good is opposed to evil, as in the quotation just above. Charles, Cathy, and Cal have bad traits opposed to the good traits of Adam and Aron. In the "thou mayest" doctrine, evil can be rejected and good chosen. (2) Good and evil are complementary. Lee thought that they might be so balanced that if a man went too far either way an automatic slide restored the balance. Good and evil are symbolized by the church and the whorehouse, which "arrived in the Far West simultaneously," and each "intended to accomplish the same thing: . . . [to take] a man out of his bleakness for a time." (3) Evil is the source of good and may even be necessary to good. The evil Cathy, quite without intending it, "set off the glory in Adam." The wealth which Cyrus Trask acquired dishonestly was inherited by Adam Trask, an honest man who used the money to rear and educate his sons. The wicked Cathy-Kate was mother of the good Aron and left her ill-gotten money to him. The "Reverend Billing" was a thief and libertine, but his sermons benefited many people. Lee said to Adam concerning Charles's bequest to Cathy, "Saints can spring from any soil. Maybe with this money she would do some fine thing. There's no springboard to philanthropy like a bad conscience." We had been told, however, that Cathy had no conscience. (4) Good and evil are relative terms. Lee said to Adam in that same speech, "What your wife is doing is neither good nor bad," although she was operating the most perverted and depraved brothel in California. This seems to hark back to Casy's doctrine: Kate's activities were simply not nice.

Good is identified both with admirable individual qualities (philanthropy, kindness, generosity, self-respect, courage, creativity) and with conventional moral goodness (sexual purity, abstinence from carnal pleasures of any kind). Evil is identified with ignoble individual qualities (meanness, cruelty, violent temper, avarice, hatefulness, selfishness), with criminal acts (murder, arson, theft, embezzlement), and with carnal pleasures, particularly sex acts; and not only with prostitution and perversions, but with sexual satisfaction in general. That is, the author appears to accept Cal's label of "bad" for his adolescent desires and impulses, and of "good" for Aron's self-indulgent purity and abstinence, and to accept Abra's use of "good" and "bad" when she says that Aron is too good for her, that she herself is not good, and that she loves Cal because he isn't good. Of course, this is the way that young people talk. But Cal and Abra are never allowed to reach a more enlightened view of "good" and "bad"; Steinbeck is using them to illustrate his thesis: that there is good and bad in everyone, and that some bad is necessary (that is, it is good to be bad); and he is understanding good and bad in their terms.

We should notice that in contrast to Steinbeck's treatment of sex in earlier novels, there is no good or healthy or lusty sexual intercourse in *East of Eden*. It is always sordid, joyless, depraved, or mercenary. The good married couples produce children, but they have no love life so far as this novel is concerned. There is a hint of passion between Cal and Abra in Chapter 54, but the curtain comes down abruptly and discreetly on the scene. In one passage Steinbeck decries human sexuality: what freedom men could have without it—only, he adds, they would no longer be human. This is not at all like the old Steinbeck who celebrated sexuality. It turns out that Steinbeck's view of good and evil is that of his mythical source: it is the Mosaic view, which is to say a legal view; particular acts are good or bad, regardless of circumstances. The earlier Steinbeck saw acts in context and evaluated them accordingly, if he evaluated them at all, dismissing the religious conception of "sin" entirely. For a novel on good and evil, *East of Eden* strangely lacks ethical insight. It is true, as I have pointed out, that its author evaluates qualities as well as acts, but they remain abstract. Adam is honest and kind, we are told; but these are negative virtues in him. In truth, virtue seems to be a function of lack of energy: pernicious anemia may account for George Hamilton's sinless life, and Adam Trask was passive, inert, non-resistant. The positive behavior of the "good" characters is at best unpleasant. Aron is selfish, inconsiderate, unloving. Adam neglects his boys for twelve years, never loves anybody except Cathy, and loves her blindly. His rejection of Cal's gift was brutal, unfeeling, and this after he had begun a cordial relationship with his son. Did Steinbeck, perhaps, intend to show that these "good" persons were not what others thought them to be? Hardly. Lee, his spokesman, said about Adam, "I think in him kindness and conscience are so large that they are almost faults. They trip him up and hinder him." Like Aron, he is too good; a man needs a little "bad" in him; you can be good if you don't have to be perfect, said Lee. We come back to moral confusion, since "good," "bad," and "perfect" are given conventional definitions, never questioned. If Steinbeck had delved into a father's ambivalent feelings for his sons, his awareness of favoring one son over the other, his fairness or unfairness to either son, and the moral and spiritual problems arising from his relation to his sons, then *East of Eden* might have been a great novel. As it is, we do not understand Adam's actions; in this novel we cannot resort to saying that they just happened.

We are indeed told that Adam could not help doing what he did. Lee said to Cal, "That's his nature. It was the only way he knew. He didn't have any choice." Why doesn't "thou mayest" apply to Adam as to other men? On his deathbed he did exercise choice by forgiving Cal with the blessing *Timshol*. Lee also said to Cal, "But you have. . . . You have a choice." And Cal then chose to get revenge on Aron. The final meaning of *timshol* for Cal is that his wicked deeds will not prevent his choosing to do good in the future.

Joseph Wood Krutch's favorable review ended with the questions: "Does the fable really carry the thesis; is the moral implicit in or merely imposed upon the story; has the author recreated a myth or merely moralized a tale?" He did not answer the questions. Our answer must be, "No. The moral is imposed upon the story, which is not a recreated myth." A reader can enjoy *East of Eden* for its many fine passages of description and many pages of skillful narrative; but the myth invoked does not adequately interpret the narrated events.

SWEET THURSDAY

From the highly serious *East of Eden* Steinbeck turned quickly to the low comedy of *Sweet Thursday,* published in the spring of 1954. It is ostensibly a sequel to *Cannery Row.* Doc, after service in World War II, comes back to Cannery Row and reopens Western Biological Laboratory. Mack, Eddie, and Hazel are still living in the Palace Flophouse with Whitey No. 1 (who was bartender at La Ida in *Cannery Row*) and Whitey No. 2. The Whiteys replace Gay (killed in the war), Hughie, and Jones. Lee Chong's store has been taken over by a rascally Mexican named Joseph and Mary Rivas. The madame of the Bear Flag is now Dora's sister Flora, called Fauna.

Doc had a hard time getting back into his old manner of life on Cannery Row; he is not only lonely now, but discontented too. He started a scientific paper called "Symptoms in Some Cephalopods Approximating Apoplexy," but could make no progress on it. What bothered him, although he did not know it, was need for a wife. Fauna and her girls and Mack and his boys immediately perceived his need and started a campaign to marry him to Suzy, a new girl at the Bear Flag, who, we are assured, was really not cut out for prostitution. Needless to say, they succeeded. But first there was a costume party at the Palace Flophouse, designed to raise money for the microscope which Doc needed and to promote a match between Doc and Suzy. As in *Cannery Row,* the first attempt to do something for Doc ended in catastrophic failure. Doc and Suzy were estranged. Hazel brought them together by breaking Doc's arm, thus arousing Suzy's affectionate sympathy. To cap the happy ending, Doc's eccentric friend, the wealthy amateur scientist called Old Jingleballicks, established Doc as director of the cephalopod research section at California Institute of Technology, so that Doc could have a good salary, write his paper, and read it at the California Academy of Sciences.

If this sounds like a musical-comedy plot, that is what Steinbeck intended. While he wrote it, Rodgers and Hammerstein were already at work upon songs and music for the stage version. The novel was easily converted into the libretto *Pipe Dream,* because it is practically a libretto as it stands. Like the several songs and musics of *The Pearl,* Doc's top, middle, and low voices, and blasts of trumpets and trombones played by the Espaldas Mojadas echo through the whole of *Sweet Thursday.* Once we realize the true nature of this book and forget about its relation to *Cannery Row,* we perceive that the Bear Flag girls are prostitutes much as the Pirates of Penzance are buccaneers. The girls turn out to be sweet bridesmaids like the chorus of *Ruddigore.* Fauna's house is really a school for brides, and Fauna's sole aim is to make good marriages for her girls: she trains them in etiquette and puts up a gold star for every marriage (she is a combination of Ma Joad, Emily Post, and fairy godmother). Mack and the boys are discovered to be property owners. The knavish Joseph and Mary Rivas is about as villainous as the last baronet of Ruddigore. A Gilbertian kind of paradox appears in Joseph and Mary's knowledge "that the only person you can trust is an absolutely selfish person," and in his conclusion that honesty might be the best racket.

Now if *Sweet Thursday* were really the gay foolery of W. S. Gilbert, we could accept its preposterous features. But on one side it is farce that often degenerates into tasteless slapstick; e.g., Hazel, in the outrageous costume designed for him by Joe Elegant, was struck by Johnny Carriaga's rubber-tipped arrow and "leaped in the air and came down on the oven door, scattering crushed ice all over the floor. One of the guests had got wedged in the grandfather clock. From the outside the Palace Flophouse seemed to swell and subside like rising bread." In that last sentence the Disney influence is visible; notice too that the costume-party theme was "Snow White and the Seven Dwarfs" in Disney's version, since we hear about Grumpy and Sweet Pea the Skunk (the entire book may be considered a Snow White or Cinderella story with Suzy in the title role and Doc as Prince Charming). On another side *Sweet Thursday* has too much of *East of Eden's* serious moral message in it, sententious statements on good and bad ("It's all part of one thing—the good and bad"), guilt, love, marriage, and individual creativity.

This serious moral undertone reveals that *Sweet Thursday* was deliberately written to reject the teaching of *Cannery Row* and replace it with a newer gospel. The first sentence of the Prologue reflects Steinbeck's purpose: Mack says, "I ain't never been satisfied with that book *Cannery Row.* I would of went about it different." The ideal is no longer the non-teleological sage, Doc of *Cannery Row,* but the good husband and organization man. Mack and the boys are still bums, but very respectable bums who promote matrimony. The attempt to combine the humorous tone of *Cannery Row* with the street's new look is singularly unsuccessful, and the mirth has a false ring. The middle-class value of having many possessions is gently ribbed ("The doctrine of our time is that man can't get along without a whole hell of a lot of stuff," says Doc), but the author lets us know that he upholds the community mores, and his thesis is that the sage needs love (as manifested in a good wife) in addition to wisdom.

As Lisca has pointed out, the old man of *To a God Unknown,* who lived by the sea and made sacrifices to the setting sun, reappears in *Sweet Thursday,* meeting Doc about forty years after his meeting with Joseph Wayne. On the beach Doc talked with the old seer, a bearded man who lived among the dunes and invited Doc to share his dinner. He pointed out to Doc the metal in the sea, as he had pointed out the metal in the mountains to Joseph Wayne; and like Joseph, Doc marvelled at the old man's mode of life (Joseph told his brother, Thomas, that the old man was crazy but not dangerous; the seer said the same thing about himself to Doc). Above all, the old man still identified himself with the sunset, saying, "I have to go to the sunset now. I've come to the point where I don't think it can go down without me." His eyes have now changed in color from black to blue, and his gospel too has changed profoundly: it is no longer the mystic unity of all things, but simply that nothing big can be done without love.

He is not the only early Steinbeck character to reappear in *Sweet Thursday:* none other than James Flower of *Cup of Gold* returns as the wealthy amateur scientist, Old Jingleballicks, who likewise scattered his interests and carried on pointless researches. As Flower "pulled the legs from numberless insects," Old Jay pulled worms from the ground with a scale held in his teeth, trying to measure "how much actual pull was involved." Each was addicted to sententious statements and strange speculations. And each was the hero's fairy godfather who staked him to the career he wanted.

Suzy is a splendid example of the Virgin Whore, as Claude-Edmonde Magny, reviewing *East of Eden,* called the mythical prototype of Steinbeck's woman as sexual object. According to Magny, the traditional Virgin Whore may be nymphomaniac or frigid; she may be Aphrodite or Artemis or Hekate; she is manifested in story as Helen or Judith or the Giftmädchen. Cathy Ames is one kind, particularly deadly; other phases appear in La Santa Roja, Teresina Cortez, Curley's wife, Mary Teller, Rose of Sharon, Molly Morden, Camille Oaks, and Mordeen. The only other kind of woman in Steinbeck's novels, according to Magny, is the wholly different maternal figure, who is nearly sexless. Although temporarily employed at the Bear Flag, Suzy struck Doc as "maidenly"; she had, he thought, "A kind of lonely and terrible modesty." At the masquerade, when Fauna shouted, "Doc, come get your girl!" it seemed to Doc, as he looked on Suzy, "a dream, a craziness, the crown, the veil, the virginity." Faulkner's recent Miss Corrie (*The Reivers*) is a chip off the same block, a whore who is strangely innocent and pure.

While old individual characters reappear, the collective character, the group organism, is barely visible. Rumors and emotions course through Cannery Row; it goes into shock and then lethargy after the terrible party—that is about all.

The contrast between *Sweet Thursday*'s cheery affirmations and *Cannery Row*'s pessimism is pointed up by the references in each novel to the poem "Black Marigolds," translated from the Sanskrit by Mathers. Doc read the poem aloud in *Cannery Row*, and he made an obvious allusion to it in *Sweet Thursday* when he said that without Suzy "I'll live a gray half-life, and I'll mourn for my lost girl every hour of the rest of my life." The title "Black Marigolds" was taken by Mathers from his epigraph, a quotation from a certain Azeddin El Mocadecci: "And sometimes we look to the end of the tale that there should be marriage-feasts, and find only, as it were, black marigolds and a silence." Steinbeck chose that *Sweet Thursday* end with marriage-feasts.

THE SHORT REIGN OF PIPPIN IV

Steinbeck's next book was in essence another musical comedy, or "frothy extravaganza," as his publishers called it. In the mid-fifties Steinbeck lived for a time in Paris with his wife and two boys, and out of that experience came some magazine articles and, in 1957, *The Short Reign of Pippin IV: A Fabrication*. It is a fantasy set in the near future, on the order of Chesterton's *The Napoleon of Notting Hill*. France reverts to monarchy and for king chooses Pippin Héristal, amateur astronomer, descendant of the Carolingians. In ten months he is overthrown because instead of allowing himself to be a "patsy" for the political parties, he has dared to be king and demand a reform program to end corruption and give equal opportunity to every citizen. Pippin went back to his astronomy, not unhappily.

In this comedy too, farce, punctuated with sententious statements, frequently descends to slapstick: Pippin's ill-fitting marshal's uniform and Miss France, representing Joan of Arc at the coronation, who "fainted from heat and the weight of her armor. She crashed with the sound of falling kitchenware during the royal oath. However, six altarboys quickly propped her against a Gothic column,

where she remained forgotten until late in the evening." The buffoon-
ish passages on French politics are equally tasteless: the confusing
interplay of political parties and forces in France is not compre-
hended in true satire, but misunderstood in coarse burlesque. French
parties are given such names as Christian Atheists, Christian Communists, Christian Christians, Conservative Radicals; political leaders are named Rumorgue, Deuxcloches, Douxpied, Veauvache, Comte
de Jour (Pasmouches is a captain of the guard). To comic-opera
Frenchmen is opposed a red-blooded American boy, son of the Egg
King of Petaluma: Tod Johnson, with whom the princess Clotilde
unaccountably falls in love. His Americanism is emphasized by giving
him such speeches as "Baby, you're a dish," "Come again?" "No
kidding!" "I'm more on the progressive kick myself"—all this in
talking to a king and princess, and after he has been to Princeton,
Harvard, and Yale. His excessively slangy speech alternates with dis-
courses on the French and American economies, which, though un-
sound, nevertheless show more knowledge than he appears likely to
have acquired. He is "well mannered," but slaps a king on the back—
I doubt that the ugliest American would do that.

Such is the comic dress of a serious theme: a ruler's decision to risk
everything for the right. But what surprises one most is the program
which brings the king's downfall: lower taxes equitably imposed on
everyone, control of wages and prices, public housing and insurance
programs, economy in government, and the break-up of large landholdings. A John Bircher might find this a socialistic program (wages
would "be keyed to profits"); but it is hardly a liberal program, since
conservatives approve very much of low taxes, government economy,
and control of wages. However we characterize this program, the fact
is that France already has had this sort of legislation for many years:
price controls, social insurance, income taxes, and the rest. France's
difficulties have not arisen from lack of such laws. The breaking up
of large landed estates was done in the French Revolution—and
Pippin's aristocratic supporters had not yet recovered their ancestors'
lands.

There is little sign of the group organism in Steinbeck's treatment
of France and French political parties. He presents them, in fact, as
unusually disunited and individualistic. Their collective emotions do
not rise spontaneously from their collective personality, but are produced artificially by clever manipulators of propaganda. Myth and
ritual may be seen, however. Pippin is the *interrex*, temporary king,
mock king. He was named king in February, and his election was

heralded by a meteoric shower; he was crowned in early summer; in autumn he ruled as king over bountiful harvests; he was dethroned in December as winter came on; and Steinbeck describes each seasonal change with something of his old power. The mock king is the carnival king, the Lord of Misrule: Pippin's clownish character is revealed in the absurd costume which he wore when he addressed the constitutional convention on December 5. Slapstick ends the astonished silence with which his speech is received. As he walks away from the rostrum his robe is ripped off, its train caught under a page boy's foot, "exposing the row of safety pins up the back of his tunic, and the baggy crotch of the trousers flopping between his knees." Then the assembly breaks into hysterical laughter. The carnival is over, the mock king is dethroned, the new year begins, and the land remains safe and secure. Remember Benjy Wayne, the scapegoat mock king of *To a God Unknown,* who was partly undressed when he was killed.

What are we to gather from this fantasy? A man does his job as well as he can, and tries to do the good that his position demands; but he does not succeed in improving the human condition, which remains comfortably corrupt. His effort is both valuable and foolish. Some men are pushers-in and others are pullers-out, as an old man told Pippin; and some play the royal fool for the welfare of the land —they are just that way.

THE WINTER OF OUR DISCONTENT

The two extravaganzas may, if we wish, be considered mere *jeux d'esprits* in which the gaiety seems rather forced. In *The Winter of Our Discontent,* his most recent novel (1961), Steinbeck returns to serious vein, apparently considering it to be his third peak of achievement. Some critics, indeed, hailed it as evidence of Steinbeck's return to high standards and significant themes. Though other critics were less enthusiastic, Dr. Anders Osterling, spokesman for the Nobel Prize Committee, mentioned *The Winter of Our Discontent* along with Steinbeck's pre-war novels as a reason for awarding him the prize.

It is meant to be a study of the moral climate of America in 1960, the decay of standards evident in payola scandals, fixed TV quiz programs, kickbacks, devious methods of making profits, and the general acceptance and approval of the "fast-buck" philosophy. Ethan's boy puts it, "Everybody does it. It's the way the cooky crumbles." The scene is New Baytown on Long Island, an old whaling port; the hero,

Wide World Photos

JOHN STEINBECK RECEIVING THE NOBEL PRIZE FROM KING GUSTAVUS VI OF SWEDEN, 1962

133

Ethan Allen Hawley, a man of singular honesty inherited from his Puritan ancestors, belongs to an old and respected family of the town, but has fallen to low estate. Bankruptcy had forced him into taking a job as clerk in the grocery store which he once owned and which had been bought by Marullo, a wealthy Sicilian immigrant. The story begins on Good Friday of 1960 and ends just after Independence Day. These dates were deliberately chosen, for the theme of corruption is expressed in terms of both Christian and patriotic ethics.

The symbolism of death and resurrection is made very obvious in Part I. The story opens with Ethan and Mary Hawley waking on Good Friday morning. When Mary reminded him of the day Ethan said, "The dirty Romans are forming up for Calvary." His employer, we soon learn, was a descendant of the ancient Roman Marulli. That day everything conspired to make Ethan discontented with his lot, after he had been tolerably satisfied in his clerkship for twelve years. Mr. Baker, the banker, urged him to recover his proper position in the community; Margie Young-Hunt contrived a prediction that he would become rich (here is the oracle of the novel); Marullo revealed the realities of business practice; a salesman offered him a bribe; Joey Morphy, the bank clerk, made cynical remarks about business practices; finally, his wife, son, and daughter complained about their poverty. As Margie left him she said, "So long, Savior!" (later Ethan called his wife "Mary, madonna"). The story of the Passion ran through Ethan's head all day. He stayed in the dark store (shades drawn) from twelve until three, troubled by the morning's events and reciting Luke's version of Christ's Passion. Early on the morning of Holy Saturday he entered a cavelike recess in the old dock beside the bay: this represents the descent into Hell on "the only day in the world's days when He is dead." Then Easter Sunday was the day of Ethan's resurrection; its meaning is related to Ethan's "change—a bloody big storm of a change." He felt renewed because he had decided to leave the narrow path of rectitude temporarily and enrich himself by shady means: he would (1) acquire the store at a low price from Marullo, whose illegal entry into the country Ethan would make known to the government; (2) acquire the desired site of the town's future airport from its alcoholic owner, his boyhood friend Danny Taylor, by lending Danny a thousand dollars, which Danny was supposed to use for a cure, but which Danny, as Ethan knew, would spend on whisky; (3) rob Mr. Baker's bank, a perfect setup for Ethan. As it turned out, Ethan did not rob the bank, as he was interrupted at the opportune moment, but he hardly needed to do so, since his two other plans were successful.

In truth, the bank-robbery motif is an unnecessary encumbrance on the plot. Its presence is due to the novel's origin in Steinbeck's short story, "How Mr. Hogan Robbed a Bank" (*Atlantic Monthly,* March, 1956), in which Mr. Hogan, obviously the original of Ethan Hawley, carried his plan of robbing a bank without "hanky-panky" to a successful conclusion. In expanding the story to novel size, Steinbeck would have done better either to stay with the bank robbery alone or to replace it entirely with the business operations.

Ethan's success in acquiring riches through sacrifice of principle became ironical when he found that Marullo, grateful to him for his consistent honesty as Marullo's clerk, had given him the store; when the essay which Ethan's son had written for a national "I Love America" contest, and which on July 4 had received honorable mention with certain rewards, turned out to be copied from Henry Clay and other American statesmen; and when it also turned out that Ethan's daughter Ellen had been the informer against her brother, thus repeating his own deed of informing on Marullo. Moreover, Danny Taylor drank himself to death with whisky that Ethan's money had bought him. Ethan resisted a temptation to commit suicide; but we do not learn whether he kept his newly acquired wealth or renounced it.

Plainly this is another example of myth inversion. It is the betrayer Judas who experiences the passion and resurrection; and he betrays Pontius Pilate. On Holy Saturday evening, when Margie was the Hawley's dinner guest, Ethan was seized by a sudden pain, which caused him to "understand how people once believed the devil could take possession." Soon afterward Margie saw in her tarot cards a rattlesnake changing its skin. Margie has an aura of witchcraft about her; much is made of her Russian grandmother who was exiled to Alaska for witchcraft. Margie, a promiscuous woman (especially for lonely, lost men)—and Mary Hawley's best friend—is plainly the Virgin Whore: "a predator, a huntress, Artemis for pants." In the Easter story she is Mary Magdalene beside Mary Madonna.

The gospel story is thus satirically inverted in order to suit it to the rituals of the true American religion of today, as Steinbeck sees it, a religion whose churches are business house and bank. When Ethan came to work on Good Friday morning, "A reflected cathedral light filled the store, a diffused cathedral light like that of Chartres. Ethan paused to admire it, the organ pipes of canned tomatoes, the

chapels of mustard and olives, the hundred oval tombs of sardines."
Ethan then chanted counterfeit Latin, "Unimum et unimorum," in
something like the Black Mass. But the grocery cathedral is nothing
compared to the bank, as Joey Morphy described it: "Comes nine
o'clock on the nose we stand uncovered in front of the holy of holies.
Then the time lock springs and Father Baker genuflects and opens
the safe and we all bow down to the Great God Currency." Joey also
referred to Baker as "God Almighty." The daily service is both
Catholic and Masonic: ". . . we open the safe like a lodge meeting.
Might as well be holding candles. It's kind of holy."

In this religion Judas is the Savior; in this tradition Richard III
is a hero. Like Richard, Ethan soliloquizes and dreams; in fact, this
is Steinbeck's first novel told in the first person (except for the first
two chapters of each part). The "glorious summer [made] by this
sun of York" following "the winter of our discontent" is American
prosperity following upon years of depression and war. But Ethan,
resident of New York, wealthiest state, does not share in this prosperity. His honesty is as discordant as Richard's malformed body,
and so, like Richard, he has "no delight to pass away the time":

> And therefore, since I cannot prove a lover,
> To entertain these fair well-spoken days,
> I am determined to prove a villain,
> And hate the idle pleasures of these days.
> Plots have I laid, inductions dangerous,
> By drunken prophecies, libels, and dreams, . . .
>
> (*Richard III*, I. i. 28–33)

As Richard's word to King Edward about a prophecy resulted in
Clarence's imprisonment, Ethan's word to the Immigration Service
resulted in Marullo's arrest. In his dream at Bosworth Field Richard
saw Clarence's ghost and heard him say,

> I, that was wash'd to death with fulsome wine,
> Poor Clarence, by thy guile betray'd to death! (V. iii. 132 f.)

In a dream Ethan saw Danny melting away and "heard his voice, distorted and thick like words spoken under water." Danny almost
literally drowned in the whisky that Ethan's money supplied him, as
Clarence was drowned in a butt of Malmsey by Richard's agents.
Thus does Steinbeck bring home to us the relevance of his title.

We have come back full circle to Henry Morgan, also a fit hero of
Currency worshippers. Ethan, the would-be bank robber, is a descendant of privateers, whom the British called pirates. Like Stein-

beck's Morgan, Ethan discovered that "honesty is the best racket": have a perfect record of probity and you can get away with anything (provided that you do it right). Ethan, however, is a reluctant Morgan, and though he attains his goal completely, his gains too are really Dead-Sea fruit.

As in his earlier novels, Steinbeck uses the myth to make an ironic comment on reality. His intention, to look at corrupt reality behind the image, is identical with that of several great novelists. The execution, however, falls short, and I share Granville Hicks's judgment: that Ethan Hawley, as Steinbeck delineates his character, would not suddenly turn to treachery and meanness; that Steinbeck does not solve the problems which he raises; and that he fails to dip beneath the surface of society: he does not probe the social and economic reasons for the decay of moral standards. "A novel indicting our low moral state," says Hicks, "ought . . . to deal with a representative person in a representative situation." Ethan Hawley is improbable, and so is his story.

We can hardly accept Ethan's transformation as just something that happened. This is not a non-teleological novel. Nor can we suppose that he is just a cell in a larger organism, taking his impulse from the larger being. For only a vestige of the group organism remains in this novel: the old families, the Hawleys and Bakers, were like the craft communities of *Burning Bright*, "a kind of nucleus walled and moated against outsiders." And we are told that communities, like people, experience health, sickness, youth, age, hope, and despair. The group organism has not been much in evidence in Steinbeck's novels for over ten years.

The writing in this novel lacks the assurance of the earlier Steinbeck. He seems to be trying too hard for profundity or beauty or humor, often descending to the merely tasteless, as when Margie Young-Hunt first appears: "Her tweed skirt clung lovingly in against her thighs and tucked up under her proud fanny, . . ." In recent novels Steinbeck has shown a tendency towards this sort of thing, and here it breaks loose. Ethan's names for Mary are equally tiresome; he has more than thirty endearing terms for her like "ladybug," "flower feet," "pigeon flake," "holy quail," even "ablative absolute." As Mary said, "You talk terrible when you're silly."

TRAVELS WITH CHARLEY

Most recently (July, 1962) Steinbeck has published his fifth book of nonfiction, *Travels with Charley in Search of America*. Believing that he had lost touch with his country, he bought a small truck with camper top and set out just after Labor Day, 1960, with Charley, an old French poodle, as his sole companion. More than one human being, he thought, would disturb the ecological balance of the regions visited. He went around the country counterclockwise, from New England across to Seattle, down to California, through the southwest to Texas and New Orleans, and quickly back to New York as Christmas drew near, a three-month tour. The published result is a series of selected incidents and encounters, sometimes entertaining or amusing, which lead to scattered reflections on various topics, somewhat as in *Sea of Cortez,* but much less profound. Steinbeck grants that his experiences add up to a chaotic mass of impressions, which he declines to sort out and put in order. His one general conclusion is that Americans are truly a distinct breed: the likenesses between sections outweigh the differences, and there is a cultural sameness everywhere— yet Texans are a distinct breed, too, different from other Americans and all other peoples. Each American is a distinct individual, but each has the distinguishing American character.

Thus, Steinbeck's organismic theory still shows through. We are also told that a trip, like a party (as in *Cannery Row*), is an individual entity, each having its own personality and temperament. The party-entity appears too: Steinbeck and eight French Canadians, gathered under the camper top and sipping cognac, became a single being, a whole with nine parts. Obviously he still likes the group-organism conception. Nor has he forsaken biology. Perhaps the best chapter is his discourse on life in the desert, the only passage in which he does more than allude to his zoological studies. There, indeed, he shows real enthusiasm as he talks about desert animals. *Homo Americanus* did not really interest him very much, and Charley is rather a bore (and how different from Doubletree Mutt).

Steinbeck called his vehicle Rocinante, and that name reveals his central symbol. He was Don Quixote, traveling about the crowded, mechanized atomic-age America of 1960, but spiritually living in a past era which he has idealized, the America of his boyhood in Salinas and Monterey County, still Victorian in outlook, when he felt the promise of American life. He tells us about his visit to Monterey in 1960. He found Johnny Garcia's bar and its proprietor; but the town was no longer the same. Commercialism, "the complicated systems of American business," have finally routed the embattled paisanos and annihilated Tortilla Flat. Cannery Row has become a tourist attraction, made so by John Steinbeck, who insists that he is a New Yorker.

10

⤔ CONCLUSION

Biology and myth provide the two poles of Steinbeck's world, tide pool and paradise. He has built a hierarchy of organisms from the individual creature up through ever larger group organisms to the whole of life and the world. We start with pure biology and end with pure myth; as we move upwards, we gradually move from the organic world to the imaginative and spiritual. At the tide pool we see Steinbeck the naturalist, realist, non-teleologist, who looks objectively and sympathetically on all forms and activities of life. Here is life as it is lived by "hurrying, fighting, feeding, breeding animals," valuable just because they are alive. It is a thoroughly democratic world, because every creature is related to every other in the very act of living. In the struggling mass of tide-pool animals not only cruelty and terror are visible, but also symbiosis, sexual attraction, rudimentary intelligence, which are the sources of friendship, love, mutual aid, and wisdom. As we rise from the tide pool through Tortilla Flat, Cannery Row, and the migrant camps, though we still see the combative and predatory characteristics of the tide pool, we see more and more cooperation, fraternity, and intelligence. The creatures of the tide pool begin to have aspirations and to reach a vision of the whole.

At the paradise extremity we see Steinbeck the mythmaker and mystic, "Naturalism's Priest," as Woodburn Ross has called him, dreamer of the American dream, which has traditionally taken the form of a vision of earthly paradise, a copy of the heavenly paradise. As Frederic Carpenter has shown, Steinbeck's novels illustrate "successive phases of the American dream," from Henry Morgan's dream of empire and wealth in El Dorado to Tom Joad's vision of a co-operative commonwealth. Paradise is involved in nearly every Steinbeck novel: the Grail Paradise and Avalon of Arthurian legend in *Cup of Gold* and *Tortilla Flat*, the asphodel fields of *The Pastures of Heaven*, the promised land of *To a God Unknown* and *The Grapes of Wrath*, the Eden of *In Dubious Battle* and *East of Eden*.

Alfred Kazin calls this paradise Happy Valley, considering it to be Steinbeck's central theme, taking the form "of some natural tradition despoiled," present also in the writings of Thoreau, Mark Twain, Norris, Faulkner, and Hemingway. That is, Steinbeck's central theme is Paradise Lost, taking various forms: illusory paradises found worthless in the attainment (*Cup of Gold, The Pearl*) or shattered by reality (*The Pastures of Heaven*), or acceptable paradises, made so difficult to achieve by the forces of property (*In Dubious Battle, The Grapes of Wrath*) or by the seekers' own failings (*Of Mice and Men*) as to be virtually unattainable; or if one succeeds in cultivating his personal garden of Eden by isolating it from the external world, one becomes inhuman ("The White Quail").

The opposing themes of Paradise and Paradise Lost reveal a deep ambivalence. Steinbeck is sympathetic to genuine human aspirations, and yet must always show them either defeated or, if attained, disappointing. He wants to say that this is the way of the world; but is his conviction based on genuine insight into social forces and individual minds, or is it a preconception, a naive acceptance of the pessimism and cynicism of literary predecessors? He has not satisfactorily reconciled paradise with the tide pool. He wants to do this by showing the unity of all life in one great panpsychic being; but the individual life turns out to be of no importance in the whole: an individual's death is necessary to the life of the group, the species, the whole. The whole is indifferent and even hostile to man's aspirations: "You are the cycle," said Joseph Wayne, "and the cycle is too cruel"—that may be the key statement in all Steinbeck's work. It is a one-sided—and even outdated—biological point of view, and it is not a satisfactory substitute for what Kazin calls a "value tradition." Steinbeck's non-teleological philosophy confuses commitment with *parti pris;* but what commitment means is attachment to and participation in a tradition, a feeling for the movement of history. In Steinbeck's novels biology takes the place of history, mysticism takes the place of humanism.

Although in the preceding paragraphs I have simply referred to

Steinbeck's novels as if I meant all of them, I have perforce been speaking mainly of his pre-war novels. We have noticed a change in his writing, especially since 1950. As if aware of something unsatisfactory in his point of view, Steinbeck turned from biology to a vague moralism, which proved even more unsatisfactory, since it was not derived from a penetrating study of men interacting in society. He saw the world more whole when he saw it biologically.

In spite of their philosophic shortcomings, the earlier novels are great novels. There is much that is good in them: accurate observation, clear and forceful writing, human sympathy, splendid insight. I am not sure that I would except *Cup of Gold* and *To a God Unknown* (the latter is really a remarkable book); I would certainly recommend them above anything that Steinbeck has written since *East of Eden* (and perhaps since *Cannery Row*). For in spite of beginner's faults they show a novelist on the way up. In all Steinbeck's novels written before 1940 myth has a dynamic function. Thoroughly integrated with the narrative theme, it serves to interpret reality and to explode romantic illusion; in later novels the myth is externally imposed on the material in an attempt to achieve the same results.

The pleasantest part of this study has been to share Steinbeck's joy in myth and legend. He has relied principally on the Arthur cycle and Biblical tales, especially the Holy Grail and Fisher King, Garden of Eden, Cain and Abel, the Joseph story, Exodus, Leviathan, the Passion and Resurrection, the revolt of the angels. They are by no means his only myths: cosmogonic myths, dying god, Faust, Troy and Helen, Virgin Whore, legends of city-founding—all these and more have had their poetic use in Steinbeck's fiction. It is myth that attaches his work most closely to the great tradition of the European and American novel.

At one time Steinbeck said that all his work was meant to help people understand one another. He has wanted to enlist our sympathy for men of all degrees, for the wise and feeble-minded, for beggars and kings alike. His most persistent theme has been the superiority of simple human virtues and pleasures to the accumulation of riches and property, of kindness and justice to meanness and greed, of life-asserting action to life-denying. In several ways he has asserted that all life is holy, every creature valuable. Herein lies his sentimentality, but also his strength. His great novels, like *The Grapes of Wrath,* will endure for their narrative power and strength of vision.

SELECTED BIBLIOGRAPHY

Note: (P) indicates works available in paperbound editions.

STEINBECK'S CHIEF WORKS

Fiction

Cup of Gold. New York: Robert M. McBride & Co., 1929. (P)

The Pastures of Heaven. New York: Brewer, Warren & Putnam, 1932. (P)

To a God Unknown. New York: Robert O. Ballou, 1933. (P)

Tortilla Flat. New York: Covici-Friede, 1935. (P)

In Dubious Battle. New York: Covici-Friede, 1936. (P)

The Red Pony. New York: Covici-Friede, 1937; The Viking Press, 1945. (P) (Included in *The Long Valley*, 1938.)

Of Mice and Men. New York: Covici-Friede, 1937. (P)

The Long Valley. New York: The Viking Press, 1938. (P)

The Grapes of Wrath. New York: The Viking Press, 1939. (P)

The Moon Is Down. New York: The Viking Press, 1942. (P)

Cannery Row. New York: The Viking Press, 1945. (P)

The Wayward Bus. New York: The Viking Press, 1947. (P)

The Pearl. New York: The Viking Press, 1947. (P)

Burning Bright. New York: The Viking Press, 1950. (P)

East of Eden. New York: The Viking Press, 1952. (P)

Sweet Thursday. New York: The Viking Press, 1954. (P)

The Short Reign of Pippin IV: A Fabrication. New York: The Viking Press, 1957. (P)

The Winter of Our Discontent. New York: The Viking Press, 1961. (P)

Nonfiction

Sea of Cortez: A Leisurely Journal of Travel and Research (in collaboration with Edward F. Ricketts). New York: The Viking Press, 1941.

Bombs Away: The Story of a Bomber Team. New York: The Viking Press, 1942. [The bomber team is a eugenically produced group organism in which each member has his individual talent and cooperates harmoniously with the whole group.]

A Russian Journal (with pictures by Robert Capa). New York: The Viking Press, 1948. [Steinbeck and Capa made a trip to Russia in the summer of 1947 to observe how the people live. They entered the country without difficulty and traveled freely over much of it. Yet it is doubtful whether Steinbeck corrected preconceptions; and he makes editorial comments that do not agree with his reported observations and experiences.]

The Log from the Sea of Cortez. New York: The Viking Press, 1951. (P) [The narrative portion of *Sea of Cortez*, with a profile "About Ed Ricketts."]

Once There Was a War. New York: The Viking Press, 1958. (P) [Steinbeck's wartime dispatches published in the New York *Herald Tribune*, June–December, 1943, articles on the individual soldier's life in the war.]

Travels with Charley in Search of America. New York: The Viking Press, 1962. (P)

PLAYS, FILM SCRIPTS

Of Mice and Men: A Play in Three Acts. New York: Covici-Friede, 1937.

The Forgotten Village. New York: The Viking Press, 1941. [Sound track of a film. A story of conflict between modern medicine and primitive superstition in a Mexican village.]

The Moon Is Down: A Play in Two Parts. New York: The Viking Press, 1943.

A Medal for Benny. Story by John Steinbeck and Jack Wagner, screenplay by Frank Butler, in *Best Film Plays—1945*, edited by John Gassner and Dudley Nichols. New York: Crown, 1946.

Burning Bright (acting edition). New York: Dramatists Play Service, 1951.

Viva Zapata. Screenplay abridged in *Argosy* (February, 1952).

Pipe Dream (musical comedy by Richard Rodgers and Oscar Hammerstein II based on *Sweet Thursday*). New York: The Viking Press, 1956.

MINOR WORKS

Short Stories, Separately Published

Nothing So Monstrous. New York: Pynson Printers, 1936. [The Junius Maltby story from *The Pastures of Heaven* with an epilogue.]

Saint Katy the Virgin. New York: Covici-Friede, 1936. [Collected in *The Long Valley*, 1938.]

How Edith McGillcuddy Met R. L. S. Cleveland: Rowfant Club, 1943. [Appeared in *Harper's* (August, 1941); collected in second *The Portable Steinbeck*, 1946.]

Nonfiction

"Their Blood Is Strong" (pamphlet). San Francisco: Simon J. Lubin Society of California, Inc., 1938. [Articles published in *San Francisco News*, October 5–12, 1936, as "The Harvest Gypsies."]

Vanderbilt Clinic (with photographs by Victor Keppler) (pamphlet). New York: Columbia & Presbyterian Medical Center, 1947.

About Ed Ricketts. Preface to *The Log from the Sea of Cortez,* pp. vii–lxvii. New York: The Viking Press, 1951.

COLLECTED WORKS

The Portable Steinbeck, selected by Pascal Covici (Foreword by Pascal Covici). New York: The Viking Press, 1943; enlarged edition (with Introduction by Lewis Gannett), 1946. (P)

The Short Novels of John Steinbeck (with Introduction by Joseph Henry Jackson). New York: The Viking Press, 1953. [*Tortilla Flat, The Red Pony, Of Mice and Men, The Moon Is Down, Cannery Row, The Pearl.*]

CRITICAL AND INTERPRETATIVE STUDIES

Full-Length

French, Warren. *John Steinbeck.* (Twayne's United States Authors Series.) New York: Twayne, 1961. (P)

Lisca, Peter. *The Wide World of John Steinbeck.* New Brunswick: Rutgers University Press, 1958. [The first full-length study of Steinbeck's fiction. Indispensable.]

Moore, Harry Thornton. *The Novels of John Steinbeck: A First Critical Study.* Chicago: Normandie House, 1939. [A pioneer work that treats Steinbeck's novels of the thirties.]

Schumann, Hildegard. *Zum Problem des kritischen Realismus bei John Steinbeck.* Halle (Saale): Niemeyer, 1958.

Tedlock, E. W., Jr., and Wicker, C. V., editors. *Steinbeck and His Critics: A Record of Twenty-Five Years.* Albuquerque: University of New Mexico Press, 1957. [An anthology of critical essays.]

Watt, F. W. *John Steinbeck.* New York: Grove Press; Edinburgh: Oliver and Boyd; 1962. (P) [A British critic's interpretation.]

Brief Studies

Gannett, Lewis. *John Steinbeck: Personal and Bibliographical Notes* (pamphlet). New York: The Viking Press, 1939.

Magny, Claude-Edmonde. "John Steinbeck's *East of Eden.*" *Perspectives USA,* 5 (Fall, 1953).

Powell, Lawrence Clark. "Toward a Bibliography of John Steinbeck." *The Colophon,* New Series, III (Autumn, 1938), 558–568.

Simon, Jean. *Le roman américain au XXe siècle.* Paris: Boivin & cie., 1950. (Pp. 159–170 on Steinbeck.)

Whipple, T. K. "Steinbeck: Through a Glass Though Brightly," in *Study Out the Land.* Berkeley and Los Angeles: University of California Press, 1943.

Wilson, Edmund. *The Boys in the Back Room: Notes on California Novelists.* San Francisco: Colt Press, 1941.

INDEX

Note: Characters and other fictional subjects in Steinbeck's works are entered in small capital letters.

Index

Index